AF323313

Social Services Administration In Hong Kong

Theoretical Issues and Case Studies

Social Services Administration In Hong Kong

Theoretical Issues and Case Studies

Editors

Chan Kam Tong & Diana Mak

World Scientific
New Jersey • London • Singapore • Hong Kong

Published by

World Scientific Publishing Co. Pte. Ltd.

5 Toh Tuck Link, Singapore 596224

USA office: Suite 202, 1060 Main Street, River Edge, NJ 07661

UK office: 57 Shelton Street, Covent Garden, London WC2H 9HE

British Library Cataloguing-in-Publication Data
A catalogue record for this book is available from the British Library.

SOCIAL SERVICES ADMINISTRATION IN HONG KONG
Theoretical Issues and Case Studies

ISBN 981-238-375-1

This book is printed on acid-free paper.

Printed in Singapore by Mainland Press

Foreword

The idea of writing a casebook was made many years ago when the programme of the Post-graduate Diploma in Social Service Administration was first introduced in 1991. The major reason of publishing a casebook on social service administration is twofold: 1) to examine some of the prominent issues affecting the social services organizations in Hong Kong in time of changes; and 2) to materialize the essential cases of different domains of social service management.

The social services in Hong Kong have undergone tremendous changes in the past years. After the subvention review by the former Cooper and Lybrand Consultancy Company Ltd., the Government of Hong Kong has introduced the Quality Assurance framework called the Service Performance Monitoring System, SPMS, Lump Sum Grant, as well as competitive bidding. Many NGOs have encountered great challenges in terms of the new administrative arrangement and cultural changes.

This book has collected a number of case studies from former students of the Master of Arts (Social Work) students whose stream of study was Social Service Administration. Many of these studies were the action learning projects conducted by them. As part of the course requirements, students have to design and implement a change project which aims at solving a particular management issue or problem in their serving organization. They have to apply the theories to the real life situation and examine some of the issues of concerns in implementing changes in the context of Hong Kong. I am grateful to some of our friends and colleagues in the social services organizations for contributing the articles.

This book takes a longer period of time to be completed than we have expected. One of the reasons is due to the difficulties in finding suitable cases. The other reason was that we wanted to have a wide variety of cases so that a more comprehensive coverage of materials could be made. We are glad the book is published eventually and we sincerely hope that this book would provide contribution to the management training for the social service administrators in Hong Kong.

Chan Kam Tong and Diana Mak

List of Contributors

AU Wai Cheung, Cliff
Mr. Au is currently Supervisor of Group Work Unit at the Yam Oi Tong. He has also worked as Fieldwork Supervisor at the Hong Kong Polytechnic University. He obtained his MA(SW) degree in Social Service Administration from Hong Kong Polytechnic University as well.

CHAN Fung Yi, Pauline
Ms. Chan is currently Instructor at the Department of Applied Social Sciences, Hong Kong Polytechnic University. She has worked in the community development services for many years before she joined the university. She obtained her MA(SW) degree in Social Service Administration from Hong Kong Polytechnic University.

CHAN Kam Tong, Tom
Dr. Chan is currently the Stream Leader of the Social Service Administration stream of the Master of Arts (Social Work) Programme. He has worked as TQM Consultant of many non-governmental organizations and hospitals on implementing total quality management in both Hong Kong and Canada.

CHAN Mei Lan
Miss Chan was formerly the TQM coordinator of the Grantham Hospital of Hong Kong. She is a nursing officer.

CHIU Ying Yin, Dominic
Mr. Chiu is currently the TQM coordinator of the Community Rehabilitation Network (CRN) of the Hong Kong Society for Rehabilitation. He is an occupational theraptist and has served at the CRN since it was first established.

HO Suk Yi, Ivy

Ms. Ho is currently a social worker at the Community Rehabilitation Network (CRN) of the Hong Kong Society for Rehabilitation . She was formerly Fieldwork Supervisor at Hong Kong Polytechnic University and has obtained her MA(SW) degree in Social Service Administration form Hong Kong Polytechnic University as well.

HO Wing Cheung, Andy

Mr. Ho is currently Supervisor of an Integrated Team at the Hong Kong Federation of Youth Groups. He obtained his MA(SW) degree in Social Service Administration from the Hong Kong Polytechnic University.

LEUNG Sau Chu

Dr. Leung is currently the Hospital Chief Executive (HCE) of the Grantham Hospital. She has very substantive experience in health education and health promotion, as well as continuous quality improvement in hospital setting.

LAM Chu Lee, Zarina

Dr. Lam is currently Consultant of the Social Welfare Department as well as Fellow of the Centre on Ageing of Hong Kong University. She was formerly Lecturer of the Hong Kong Polytechnic University. Being commissioned by the Health and Welfare Bureau and the Social Welfare Department, she has conducted study in reviewing the home help services in Hong Kong and providing training in MDS Accreditation.

LAM Wan Cheung, Winnie

Miss Lam is now a social worker at the Social Welfare Department. She is currently enrolling the MA(SW) Programme specializing in Social Service Administration.

MAK Ping Sze, Diana

Professor Mak is currently Professor and Head of Department of Applied Social Sciences, Hong Kong Polytechnic University. She has served as a member of the University Grant Committee (UGC) and now appointed as member of the Social Welfare Advisory Committee (SWAC). She has provided consultancy services and advices to many social welfare organizations in Hong Kong.

***MOK** Tai Kei, Henry*

Dr. Mok was formerly Associate Professor of Department of Applied Social Sciences, Hong Kong Polytechnic University and a former Professor at the Department of Social Work, Baptist University. He has taught the subject Program Evaluation during his service at the Hong Kong Polytechnic University.

***SZE** Yuk Hiu, Alan*

Mr. Sze was a research associate and currently Lecturer of the Department of Applied Social Sciences of the Hong Kong Polytechnic University. He was trained in economics in both undergraduate and masters levels at the University of Hong Kong. His research interest focuses on social security and institutional development in both China and Hong Kong.

***SZETO** Wai Chu, Rachel*

Miss Szeto is now working as an Officer at the Anti-discrimination Commission. She was formerly served as an Assistant Division Officer of the Hong Kong Council of Social Service. She obtained her MA(SW) degree in Social Service Administration from the Hong Kong Polytechnic University.

***TSOI** Yuen Kan*

Ms. Tsoi is currently the Supervisor of the Medical Social Service of the United Christian Hospital. She obtained her MA(SW) degree in Social Service Administration from the Hong Kong Polytechnic University.

***YUEN** Chi Chuen*

Mr. Yuen is currently a social worker at the Social Welfare Department. He has obtained a Post-graduate Diploma in Social Service Administration from the Hong Kong Polytechnic University.

Contents

Part III   Prologue

Part I
Theoretical Issues in Social Services Administration

1

Prominent Issues Affecting Non-Governmental Organizations in Hong Kong and Its Implications to Social Work Education

CHAN Kam Tong

Introduction

In recent years, the Non-Governmental Organizations (NGOs) in Hong Kong are facing tremendous challenges and demands from both the external environment and internal administrative mechanisms. The objectives of this paper are: (i) to examine the prominent issues affecting the social welfare sector and the NGOs in Hong Kong; (ii) to examine the challenges or difficulties encountered by the social service administrators; and (iii) to discuss, with the experience of students from the post-graduate programme in social service administration at the Hong Kong Polytechnic University — how social work education responds to the ever-changing demands of the society.

Prominent Issues affecting the NGOs in Hong Kong

In recent years, social mandates on social service organizations in Hong Kong have been re-defined due to changes in social values, introduction of new ordinances, administrative rulings, and technological knowledge. The prominent issues affecting the NGOs are identified as follows:

At Societal Level

1. Changes of Political Environment

Hong Kong has faced a great political change in 1997 as the sovereignty has been returned to the Mainland China. It is perceived that there are many differences in both the conceptions and administrative system of social welfare in Hong Kong and in China. For example, the welfare of people is taken care of mainly by the work units (dan wei) in China, while the welfare needs of the Hong Kong people are being taken care of by the Social Welfare Department and NGOs. The diversity in the conception and delivery of welfare services would certainly create issues of concern for policy-makers and administrators.

2. Value for Money

This refers to stringent controls on expenditures by legislatures and executive budget offices. The slogan "do more for less" has been increasingly demanded of most of the administrators in human services. Formerly, the senior government officers from the Mainland China have also criticized the rapid increase of social welfare expenditure in the past few years. A threatening metaphor cited as "the car would be crashed and the passengers would die" may imply the decline of public expenditure in social welfare after the change of the political sovereignty.

3. Subvention Review Exercise by the Government

In April 1995, the Social Welfare Department (SWD) introduced the Subvention Review Exercise that included the proposed implementation of "Service Quality Monitoring System, SPMS" and the "Lump Sum Grant" as the approach for calculating funding to NGOs in the future. Such an exercise attempts to re-examine the current funding arrangement and the partnership between Government and the welfare sector. Service contracts between the funder (SWD) and the service provider (NGOs) are recommended as the future mode of operation in the subvention policy.

In addition, the NGOs are also required to conform to a list of performance standards, which are categorised into four major dimensions, namely: (1) provision of information; (2) service management; (3) clients' management; and (4) respect for clients' right. 19 (later reduced to 16) standard statements and 79 criteria have also been established. A service agreement would also be introduced in order to stipulate the expectations and requirements from the funder. Such a move calls for a shift of the former "partnership" relationship to a "contractual" relationship between the Government and the welfare sector. Questions and doubts about inter-dependence between the two parties would be raised.

At Organizational level

4. Use Involvement and Client Empowerment

The introduction of the Privacy Act and the Registration Bill also induces the rise of user involvement and the rights of clients in service delivery. It also reflects a different perception of relationship between the worker (service provider) and the clients (customers). Such a movement have an explicit political dimension, including the approach employed to obtain influences, as well as the aims to achieve both individual and collective empowerment over all aspects of the lives (Wistow & Barnes, 1993). The approaches in client empowerment include:

- Providing information to users;
- Obtaining opinion from users on levels of satisfaction of services;
- Developing partnerships with users in decision;
- Enabling user control of both problem definition and service delivery.

Customer accountability would become another issue of concerns for both administrators and practitioners.

5. Quality Movement

Quality is the totality of features, or characteristics, of a service that bear on its ability to satisfy a given need. It must be explicitly designed and built into a service, it cannot be inspected at the time of, or after, delivery. For quality assurance, it is the prevention of quality problems through planned and systematic activities (including documentation). These will include the establishment of a good quality management system, and the assessment of its adequacy, the audit of the operation of the system, and review of the system itself. Three key elements are considered as important:

- Fitness for purpose;
- Responsiveness to the needs of users; and
- Conformity to specification.

However, questions about the relevance of quality movement to social service are commonly raised by social workers. They would have doubts about the basic philosophy and objectives of the quality movement and query if such business-oriented initiatives are applicable to human service, since there is an absence of market mechanism.

6. Rise of Managerialism

Managerialism is about structure, order, forceful activity, and rationality. It is about hardware and technique. It does not emphasize values or how this climate affects the people who are the subject group, that is, the public, clients, and workers. The focus would then be much of the efforts and attention or retrenchment, efficiency, cost control. New technologies, some of them from business management, are deemed necessary. For example:

- Utilization management / Workload Measurement System;
- Programme / Matrix Management; and
- Quality Planning.

All these technologies are becoming important for administrators in order to enhance the efficiency and effectiveness of the organizations.

Challenges for the Administrators

In face of such a development, the functions and tasks of administrators have become increasingly complex. These tasks must be performed through a series of inter-locking processes grounded on solid value premises. Sarri (1994) points out the challenges for the social service administrators in the 90s in the US context and some of the challenges are also relevant to the situations in Hong Kong:

1. What should be the response to the pressure for greater demands for cost-efficiency so that the value bases of fairness, humanity and equity can be assured?
2. How to encourage innovative leadership and risk-taking change as a strategy for keeping the organization dynamic and responsive?
3. How to establish networking and inter-organizational collaboration through coalition building in order to "expand the boundary"for resource mobilization?
4. How to motivate the staff so that they are responsive to the changing conditions and new challenges?
5. How to design the information system at both policy and locality levels in order to serve clients, and to inform administrators so that accountability and quality control can be achieved, and the performance of the organization can be improved continuously.

Implications to Social Work Education

Beyond Rationality: *The need for a value-based paradigm in social work education?*

The increase in size and complexity of the welfare programmes, the competition for resources allocation, the changing clientele needs and the rapidly developing needs and the rapidly developing society, confront the administrative leaders with a broad range of competencies and a creative approach to problem-solving. The implications to the training of competent social service administrators should include the following four main dimensions:

1. The importance of self-understanding and self-critic as human service professionals (personal dimension);
2. The ability to examine the inter-relationship of:
   - policy and organization
   - organization and self
   - theory and practice
   - social work and social sciences (personal dimension);
3. The competence to recognise the influence of cultural impact on social phenomenon and intervention by the workers (cultural dimension);
4. The upholding and strong beliefs in their values of social justice and respect for human dignity and individual rights (moral dimension).

Illustration: The Case of Social Service Administration Programme at the Hong Kong Polytechnic University

There are various approaches to design a curriculum of social service administration based on different educational philosophy and learning goals. One significant step towards the development of a comprehensive, organized framework for social work management curriculum was taken by Patti (1977) and Slavin (1977). Both of them dealt with the content areas of the curriculum. Patti pointed out these areas and presented a formidable repertoire of knowledge, skills, values and attitudes.

Regarding the approaches to organizing the curriculum content, two of the prominent ones are as follows:

1. Pflanczer and Mirinaoff (1977) identified curricula from the perspective of skills which is defined as "abilities that can be developed and that manifest themselves in performance." They classified management skills into three types, namely personal, technical and systematic.
2. Gummer (1988) suggested three major content areas for social administration, namely policy development and implementation, managerial technologies and social service technologies. He argued that emphasis given to each of these areas should differ according to the level of administrative practice, and the contingency approach should be used to determine the most appropriate mix of the areas.

However, the above models are considered as putting too much emphasis on the skills and technologies, while the parts on the values and ethical issues are not mentioned. In designing the curriculum to enable the administrators in facing the turmoil and uncertainties, the *Competing Value Model* as developed by Quinn (1988) is adopted as the organizing framework. The approach suggests that the selection of various criteria of effectiveness reflects competing choice. The value dilemma is something which frequently confronts social work administrators who must function in an environment of multiple constituencies and competing demands. The models address the multi-dimensional rather than uni-dimensional approach. Secondly, the model also emphasises the trait and behaviour of social service administrators in coping with the dilemma. Four skills identified are: boundary-spanning skill, directing skills, human relations skills and co-ordinating skills.

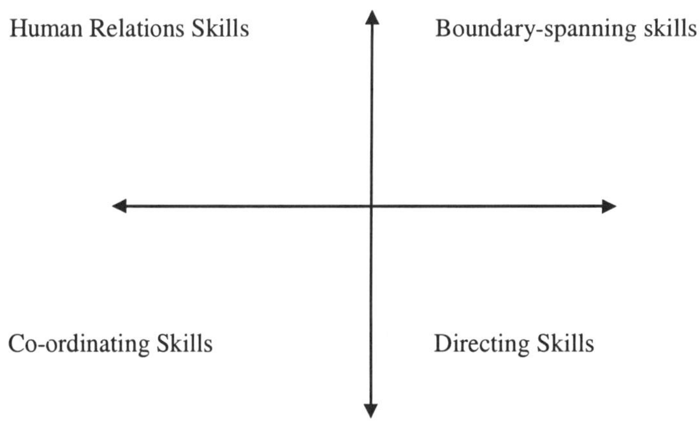

Diagram 1. Four domains of human services skills.

Course Aims: The "3Cs" Principle

With insight from the above models and approaches, the fundamental educational philosophy of the post-graduate programme in Social Service

Administration is concerned with contextualization, competence, and contingency. As discussed in previous paragraphs, the contextual environment of the administrative practice is crucial. Students should have the critical and analytical ability to discriminate and examine the real life situations and forces confronting them. They should possess the ability to distinguish between the underpinning variables which affect events and avoid the risk of overgeneralizations. Regarding competence, the students are expected to acquire the essential learning competency and practice to be prominent administrators. They should become proactive learners, gain their knowledge and uphold their values through reflective thinking and conceptualization of experience. They are also expected to acquire the practice competency at operational, interpersonal and organizational levels. By adopting the contingency view, the students are required to be creative and flexible, but grounded on a strong value base in social work, to examine the strengths and weaknesses, as well as threats and opportunities. The students are expected to develop the confidence and independence to manage in time of turbulence and uncertainty and yet stand firm in facing the conflicting values in society.

The contents and organization of the curriculum, based on the 3Cs principle are summarized as follows:

1. **Contextualization**	Social Context and Ethics Social Policy Analysis and Social Accountability	
2. **Competence**	Organizational Theories and Analysis Skills for Social Service Administration Supervision and Professional Development ProgrammeEvaluation Managing Information in Social Service Organizations Research Methods	
3. **Contingency**	Action Learning Project and the Management Workshop	

Social Context and Ethics

The subject aims at developing an understanding of the social and political changes in contemporary Hong Kong society, identifying the nature and scope of problems associated with the changing context, the social work profession as well as social service administration.

Social Policy Analysis and Social Accountability

The subject is designed to develop a sound knowledge base and insight of the theories and models in social policy formulations and analysis. It adopts a policy research orientation which is to sharpen students' ability to examine various policy issues, and to evaluate the impact of policy on society.

Organizational Theories and Analysis

The subject will focus on organizational theories and analysis and to sharpen students' understanding on the organizational relationship with outside environment and internal processes.

Skills for Social Service Administration

This subject helps students recognize the essential skills in programme management and resource management. Topics include total quality management, case management, and financial management.

Supervision and Professional Development

The subject aims at enhancing students' knowledge and skills in human resource development, especially focusing on the idea of continuing professional development (CPD).

Programme Evaluation

The subject aims at sharpening students' understanding in examining the effectiveness and efficiency of service programme in order to ensure accountability.

Management Information for Social Service Organizations

This subject examines the information needs in social service organizations, and also discusses the key concepts in designing information system in social service organizations.

Research Methods

The subject aims at introducing various qualitative and qualitative methods in analyzing social and administrative issues. It also aims to enable students to acquire a "re-search" mind in examining daily problems.

Action Learning Project & the Management Workshop

This workshop is an integrative venue which aims at connecting theory with practice. Real life situations in daily practice will examine the use of "Action Learning Project". The format is that each student is required to identify a real problem as the focus of study. They are requested to analyze the causal and correlative factors, and to recommend solutions to problem situations. What is more important, they need to articulate and conceptualize the problems and examine the value issues involved in the decision making process, as well as the "person in context" dilemma.

Conclusion

With the evolution of the local political and social system in the 21st century, it is expected that there will be further shifts in social mandates and in resources. Administrators in social organizations will be functioning in an atmosphere of tension and uncertainty, created by a combination of heightened demands for service delivery, and raising expectations for accountability and shortage of manpower. In short, they may have to operate in the face of the dilemma of providing quality service to clients and community and a broad range of competencies, both in practice and learning, and a creative approach to problem-solving is deemed necessary.

References

Edwards, R.L. & Gummer, B. (1988) "Management of Social Services: Current Perspectives and Future Trends" in Keys, P. & Ginsberg, L.H. *New Management in Human Service*, NASW Press.

Quinn, R.E. (1988) *Beyond Rational Management*, San Franciso: Jossey-Bass.

Sarri, R.C. (1992) *"Managing Human Services in Turbulent Time: Challenges for the 1990s"*, unpublished paper.

Weiner, W.E. (1982) *Human Services Management: Analysis and Application*, Illinois, Dorsey Press.

Winstow, G. & Barnes, M. (1993) "User Involvement in Community Care: Orgins, Purpose and Applications" in *Public Administration* Vol. 71, Autumn 1993, pp. 279–299.

2

The Dynamic Relationship among Different Functions of Supervision

YUEN Chi Chuen

Introduction

Supervision, just like casework, groupwork and community work, is a topic well known to all social workers. When we receive social work training, we know that there will be a supervisor supervising us in the field placement. When we take up a job in the social work field, we know that the officer-in-charge will supervise us. Until you have reached the top position in an agency, supervision will always be with you.

Supervision is also one of the elements differentiating social work profession from the medical profession. When a medical officer, not a trainee, makes a decision independently in a hospital, he will wonder why a social work officer has to get approval from the latter's supervisor for making a decision. The contrast between these two professions is actually shared by a medical officer with me at the Castle Peak Hospital. At that time I could tell the medical officer nothing but I only felt that supervision in social work plays an important role irrespective of promotion, service delivery, training and accountability.

Functions of Social Work Supervision

Actually, supervision in social work incorporates various functions that inter-mingle in a complicated manner. Kadushin (1985) recognizes three major functions of supervision. They are educational, administrative and supportive functions. The goal of educational function is to "dispel ignorance and upgrade skill" while administrative functions are to "insure adherence to policy and procedure" and supportive ones to "improve morale and job satisfaction" (Kadushin, 1985, pp. 21). I summarized his description of these three functions in the table below:

Functions	Nature	Focus	Materials	Power	Value
Administrative	Instrumental	Ability	Organizational Structure & Agency Resource	Position, Reward & Coercion	Efficiency
Educational	Instrumental	Ability	Knowledge & skills	Expertise	Competence
Supportive	Expressive	Motivation	Psychological & Interpersonal Resource	Reference	Compassion & understanding

The Complementary Relationship Among the Functions of Supervision

In the view of Kadushin, these three functions are complementary. Administrative supervision, taking care of staff's instrumental needs, provides the structure directed towards the agency goal. Educational supervision, also taking care of instrumental needs, provides the training that enables workers to achieve it. Supportive supervision, taking care of staff's expressive needs, reduces the stress from working towards the goal. Diagram 1 illustrates their relationship.

In diagram 1, three functions of supervision are related in a complementary manner and their joint effort is directed towards the organizational goal. The organizational goal here is simply defined as rendering social work service so as to meet the needs of clients. Their relations can be described in six paths from 1 to 6 in pairs.

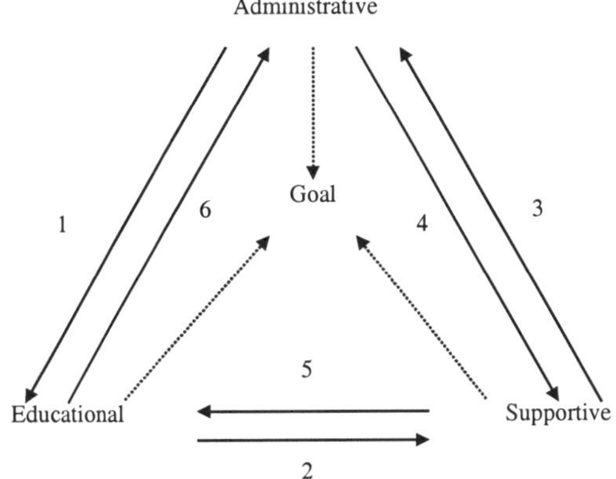

Path 1 = Set standards for learning
Path 2 = Reduce the stress from ignorance
Path 3 = Enhance compliance with sense of belonging
Path 4 = Rewarding and resource allocating
Path 5 = Create a climate for learning openly
Path 6 = Internalizing agency value, aims and procedures

Diagram 1

Path 1 and Path 6

The administrative function, with reference to the organizational goal, sets the standards for performance. From the variation between the standards and the performance of a staff member, the needs of education or training are defined. The educational function, besides fulfilling the training needs, also socializes the staff to accept the organizational goals, standards to performance, culture and other aspects.

Path 2 and Path 5

The educational function provides the staff with knowledge and skills through training. With improved knowledge and skills, the staff's stress arising from ignorance in delivery of service can be reduced. The supportive function can reduce the stress in the change of work habit or thinking pattern, which creates an adequate climate enhancing the educational function.

Path 3 and Path 4

The administrative function provides rewards to the staff with good performance and also resources to facilitate delivery of service. Obviously, this helps to reassure the staff about the support from the organization. The supportive function increases the morale and sense of belonging, which enhance compliance to the organizational aims and standards.

The Conflicts Between the Functions of Supervision

It is argued that the relations these three functions are not only complementary. They also create conflict with each other, especially between administrative and educational functions and between administrative and supportive functions. The diagram below indicates their relationship as follows:

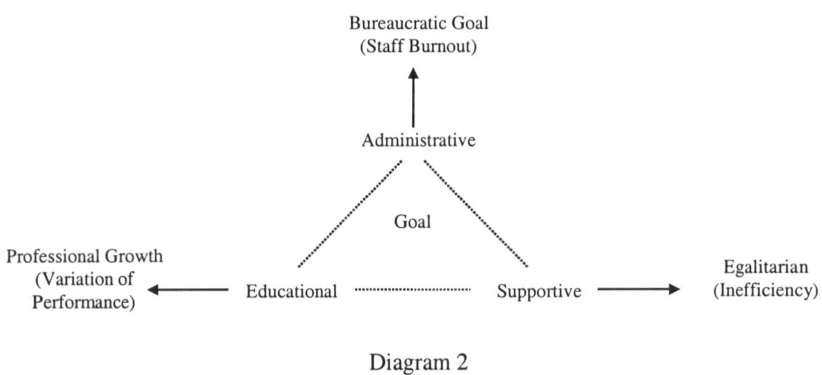

Diagram 2

The diagram indicates that three functions of supervision can have their own goals which may be compatible with the organizational goal. The administrative function can direct its effort towards the bureaucratic goal only. The bureaucratic goal materializes when the organizational goal is displaced by the formal procedures, formalities and fixed standards. One of the possible shortcomings of this administration-directed supervision is the burnout of professional staff as they are treated as interchangeable units being guided to meet standardized performance criteria (Bunker and

Wijinberg, 1988). The educational function can direct its effort towards professional growth alone. One of the possible shortcomings is the variation of performance among staff members without the control for accountability. Finally, the supportive function can direct its effort towards egalitarianism or brotherhood. Without a clear role and communication through formal relationships among staff members, inefficiency is one of the possible shortcomings.

Contrasting diagrams 1 and 2, we find that the relations among the three functions of supervision are not only complementary but also mutually constrained. In order to achieve the organizational goal, the three functions have to constrain each other and at the same time complement each other. If one of the functions has gone too far from the organizational goal, two other functions have to be strengthened to steer the balance lest the organizational goal be overlooked and the adverse side-effect emerge. Therefore, the three pairs of paths not only indicate the complementary relationships but also the mutually constrained relationships among them.

Administrative Function versus Educational Function

Paths 1 and 6 may be the pair which brings about most controversies. First of all, the educational function will sometimes be overshadowed by the administrative function. The professional growth can only be a ritual in the bureaucratic system. In some organizations, some staff members know that attending a training course is a ritual that has to be reflected in the annual appraisal report. No matter what the training need is and whether the course is really able to enhance the performance, attending a course is important to indicate a worker's "commitment" or "ambition". Even supervisors hold similar attitudes towards recommending their supervisees to attend courses.

Second, whether a supervisor can handle both the administrative and educational functions is controversial. Performing the administrative function, a supervisor has to keep evaluating the supervisee's performance with reference to the rules, regulations and standards built within the bureaucracy. Those rules, regulations and standards are relatively fixed. However, while performing the educational function, a supervisor has to teach the supervisee with relatively flexible standards. We believe that teaching is effective through encouragement and when it does not induce anxiety. To perform both of the roles, a supervisor will experience conflict between the roles.

As a student supervisor, I also experience this role conflict. In the process of teaching, assessments are ongoing and inevitable. I accept the existing performance level of a student and at the same time encourage him to make progress. I expect the student to hold an open attitude to discuss his own problems. Knowing his problems, I would suggest a learning plan (or learning contract) for him and negotiate with him about it. His progress would be an indicator of the effort he has put in for his learning. The performance level the student manifests would serve only as a reference for considering subsequent learning plans. However, a formal evaluation is quite different from such assessments. The result of the formal evaluation is used far beyond the aim of education. The result would influence the following life chances of the student, besides influencing the subsequent learning plan. Therefore, I do not think that such a formal evaluation fulfils totally an educational function. It serves as an administrative function as well. The student's performance will be judged by some standards no matter how the standards are formulated. In this process, defence from the student is quite natural. The supervisor's task is to deal with the defence and not to prevent its occurrence.

In my supervising experience, one of my students clearly spoke out about the conflict between the administrative function and the educational function. He said that in the previous learning experience, if he could make a substantial progress, he would be appreciated. However, he felt that this field placement is like an examination because his performance is judged with standards irrespective of his progress. This different experience made him feel burdensome. Sometimes, he felt confused. On one hand, he was invited and encouraged to discuss frankly about his pessimistic views on the mental health field and to consider the influence from such a view. On the other hand, in the formal evaluation, his professional intervention is judged to be handicapped by such pessimistic views. Although examples of his performance in handling cases support my judgement, he wonders whether he has been trapped. Perhaps I could have handled the situation better, but I would like to point out that the conflict between educational and administrative function is inherent.

In view of the mentioned conflict between administrative and educational functions, it is proposed that the two functions be separated. One supervisor may have difficulties performing both the functions. However, Kadushin considered that the separation of administrative and educational functions "may create greater problems than the supposed disease" because "the learning needs of the individual worker can be best discerned by the administrative supervisor who is responsible for careful review of the worker's performance" (Kadushin, 1985, pp. 483). On the contrary, Harris and Allison developed a strategy for separating the functions in the social work department of a teaching hospital (Harris & Allison, 1982). They made use of group conference, peer supervision groups, short-term seminars, consultations, staff development programs and staff's attendance at outside activities to perform the educational function.

Working in the Social Welfare Department of Hong Kong, I feel that the separation of the administrative and educational functions exists in an implicit manner. I have worked with three supervisors in the past four years in the department. I consistently find that they perform mainly the administrative functions rather than the educational functions. Monitoring the development of the cases I handle, they will remind me some important points I have to pay attention to. They will also suggest the proper way to handle some cases. However, these suggestions and reminders aim at the administrative accountability more than professional growth. For my professional growth, one of the supervisors nominated me to attend the courses organized by the Lady Trench Training Centre. Another has attempted to organize case conferences and informal seminars to meet supervisees' need for professional growth. The last one, I think, has done little about the educational functions.

However, in the department, there is a culture that the senior workers will offer guidance for the junior workers. Senior workers indeed perform the educational functions of supervision. There are advantages for senior workers to perform the function. First, senior workers will not perform any administrative function of evaluating junior workers. Therefore, junior workers can learn from them without any worry about being judged or their career being affected. Second, senior workers are also front-line workers. They can offer the most updated knowledge and skills in the delivery of services. Third, as the senior workers have no competitive relationship with junior workers, the communication between these two parties will not be distorted by prejudices. Although this practice is not formally set up, this informal practice enhances the educational functions of supervision. This practice is similar to peer supervision groups as developed by Harris and Allison.

Nevertheless, if this practice can gain support from the supervisor, who will perform the administrative function of supervision separately, this practice can be more effective. The supervisor, through monitoring supervisees' work, can point out the learning needs of supervisees. Courses organized by the Lady trench Training Centre can, of course, offer additional assistance to the professional development of the staff.

Administrative Function versus Supportive Function

Paths 3 and 4 are also a pair which easily creates trouble. From time to time, I hear some colleagues complained that their supervisors did not treat them in such a way as they are required to treat clients. They think that the supervisor, as a social worker too, should treat them in the way he treats clients. Performing administrative function, the supervisor has to ensure that the supervisee is being compliant to the requirements or standards of the agency. However, when the supervisor requires the supervisee's compliance, the former will often criticize the latter for not being supportive. Therefore, one of my friends, now taking up the position as a supervisor, told me that he is always prepared to be criticized by his supervisee if he wants the quality standards being met. As mentioned by Kadushin (1985), there are many supervisees' "games" playing in the context of this pair of paths. Supervisees can overshadow the administrative function with supportive function by lowering the demand levels, redefining the supervisory relationship, etc. As a student supervisor in the field placement, I am also criticized by my student of not being supportive when I require him to attain a certain level of performance irrespective of the difficulties he claims. To get the student's appreciation, what I have to do is to show empathy to the difficulties he meets and then adjust the requirements correspondingly. However, when I consider the administrative accountability, I show that while I understand his difficulties, he still has to meet the standards for his performance. The student, quite obviously, is not satisfied with my answer.

Another example of the conflict between administrative and supportive function concerns peer group support. Peer group support is a resource of support which enhances the supportive function. However, would you allow the staff to spend much time during office hours to discuss personal affairs? Discussions between informal relationships among staff members may be a source of support. Nevertheless, spending much time in such discussions can violate the administrative accountability. In fact, different supervisors have different standards to keep a balance. One of my supervisors once led colleagues to visit another colleague in the hospital during office hours. Another supervisor dislikes supervisees' chatting during office hours. These two supervisors have taken quite different views of the emphasis on peer group support. This difference clearly indicates the possible conflict between administrative and supportive functions of supervision.

Factors Influencing the Emphasis on the Function of Supervision

Having analyzed the dynamic relations of the three functions of supervision, I would like to discuss the factors influencing them. Those factors will be divided into categories including organizational, supervisor, task and supervisee factors.

I.   Organizational factor

It is not surprising that in a bureaucratic organization like the Social Welfare Department, administrative function will have the priority over other functions. The Social Welfare Department has a clear hierarchical structure. The formalities are also important to the communication with other governmental departments. As most of the resources of the department comes from taxpayers, the adequacy in handling resources is highly monitored. In such an organizational context, the administrative accountability will be stressed much more than the elements of professional growth. The administrative function will have the priority over the other functions.

II.   Supervisor factor

First of all, not all skillful social workers are good supervisors because the demands for a competent social worker and that for a competent supervisor are different. Second, the supervisor's personality or behavioural pattern is also a remarkable factor influencing the emphasis on which function of supervision. My students consider that my working as a probation officer is a factor contributing to my holding relatively strict standards to measure their performance. In fact, I cannot totally disregard the correlation between my daily work style and the style of supervision.

III.   Task factor

The specific requirement of a task will also influence the emphasis on the functions. The Social Welfare Department provides not only services relating to social work profession but also services relating to the legal system. Probation work and protection of children are two obvious examples of services relating to the legal system. Because there are legal responsibilities in handling cases, administrative accountability is very important. It may be more important than the elements of professional growth. In such a case, the emphasis on the administrative function of supervision is easily expected.

In addition, the different levels of tasks also require different emphasis on the functions of supervision. For minor or nonprofessional work, the supervisior mainly performs the administrative and supportive functions. The procedures of completing the tasks will be clearly discussed and compliance to the procedures and the stress in handling the job will be the main concern in the supervision. For professional workers, the educational function will be also an important function in the supervision.

IV.   Supervisee factors

Of course, the approach which the supervisee adopts towards his daily work is an important factor influencing the emphasis on different functions of supervision. If a supervisee views himself as merely instrumental in his work, he would only expect administrative supervision. The supervisee would be satisfied with his performance having met the fixed standards and he would not expect more than that from his job. However, with a developmental view towards his work, he would surely not be satisfied only with administrative supervision. Educational and supportive supervision would be demanded.

These four categories of factors influence a supervisor's choice of the emphasis on the functions of supervision interactively. Supervision style is thus a product influenced by these factors in the context of both complementary and tense relationships among the functions of supervision.

Conclusion

The three functions of supervision — administrative, educational and supportive functions — have complementary relationships with each other. However, they also constrain each other with tension in an attempt to achieve the organizational goal. Moreover, which function of supervision would be emphasized in practice is influenced by factors including organizational, supervisor, task and supervisee factors. Supervisory style is formulated with reference to these influencing factors and in the context of the dynamic relations among the three functions.

References

Bunker D.R. & Wijnberg M.H. (1988) *Supervision and Performance: Managing Professional Work in Human Service Organizations.* London: Jossey-Bass Inc.

Harris D.V. & Allison E.K. (1982) "Performance management and professional development as separate functions of supervision" in *Health and Social Work,* **7**, pp. 283–291.

Kadushin, A. (1985) *Supervision in Social Work.* New York: Columbia University Press.

3

Evaluating Social Work Effectiveness: An Illustration from a Comparative Evaluation of Three Labour Education Programs in Hong Kong

MOK Tai Kei, Henry

Introduction

Nowadays, no social work administrator nor practitioners could afford to disregard the importance of program evaluation, as there is a growing international trend towards better accountability and greater competition for cost-effectiveness. In fact, in Hong Kong, over one hundred voluntary welfare agencies were urged by the Social Welfare Department of the Hong Kong Government in as early as 1975 to use an evaluative measure to ensure quality of social work services (Social Welfare Department, 1976). However, due to the lack of readiness and expertise on program evaluation, the voluntary sector was very resistant to any form of official evaluation of their agency services. There were a few well-established welfare agencies which did conduct one or two unpublished self-evaluation on agency administration or service programs in the 1980s. It was only until 1991 that the Hong Kong Government (1991) reiterated the importance of service program evaluation through the announcement of the fourth social welfare policy paper. The Social Welfare Department (1994) has determined to assume a vigorous monitoring and evaluation role, as clearly reflected by the appointment of an independent research body to conduct service evaluation for the implementation of the Integrated Service Delivery Model of youth work in 1994.

However, despite the determination of the Hong Kong Government to demand service evaluation and to achieve better value for money, a majority of the voluntary sector is not ready to go for program evaluation. Hence it is the purpose of this paper to describe a process of a small-scale social work program evaluation and highlight some of the issues involved. It is hoped that both administrators and practitioners would be able to acquire a better understanding of evaluation and adopt a positive attitude towards evaluation study in the future.

Nature of Evaluation

There are many definitions of evaluation. In my view, Attkisson & Broskowski (1978) have arrived at a concise and comprehensive definition of evaluation:

> "A process of making reasonable judgements about program effort, effectiveness, efficiency and adequacy, based on systematic data collection and analysis, which focuses especially on accessibility, acceptability, awareness, availability, comprehensiveness, continuity, integration and cost of services, and is designed for use in program management, external accountability and future planning."

In general, a common practice of program evaluation usually includes the following major areas of research questions (see Mok, 1982):

1. Program Planning: What is the need, the extent and distribution of the target population? Is the program designed in conformity with its intended goals?
2. Program Monitoring: Is the program reaching the persons or other target units to which it is addressed? Is the program providing the resources, services or other benefits that were intended in the project design?
3. Program Effectiveness: Is the program effective in achieving its intended goals? Can the results of the program be explained by some alternative processes that are not included in the program?

4. Program Efficiency: What are the programmatic input to deliver services and benefits to program participants? Is the program an efficient use of resources compared with alternative uses of the resources?

Since most of the stakeholders including funders, professionals, clienteles and administrators are very much concerned with whether or not program goals are achieved, the following discussion focus mainly on evaluating program effectiveness.

Evaluation Program Effectiveness

To assess program effectiveness is one of the most important and common practices of evaluation. Due to limited space and time, the discussion will focus on the nature of effectiveness and the methodological steps in assessing effectiveness.

The concept of evaluation on effectiveness is best stated by Suchman as "the determination (whether based on opinions, records, subjective or objective data) of the results (whether desirable or undesirable, transient or permanent, or part of a program, an ongoing or one-shot approach) designed to accomplish some valued goals or objectives (whether ultimate, intermediate, or immediate, effort or performance, long or short range)" (1967, p. 32). This conception was adopted in evaluating citizen participation achievement of a Social Security Consortium in Hong Kong (Mok, 1987). Program effectiveness here is also concerned with the extent to which program objectives have been achieved.

Comparative Evaluation

Most evaluations are done on individual program basis. A single program evaluation is confined to observing effects at one time at one place, with a particular group of staff using a particular strategy to obtain program results. It is difficult to know how far the program effect can be generalized to other situations.

If control groups, instead of receiving no service, receive the conventional type of program strategy, the results of the study can indicate whether a new program is superior to the old. Based on this methodological design and reasoning, evaluation research could be designed with the same set of outcome measures to compare the effectiveness of several programs that have the same objectives but different working strategies. This form of comparative evaluation will increase in generalizability of results and in the specification of which working strategy under which conditions has better effects (Weiss, 1972). The ability to isolate factors that work is a major contribution of comparative evaluation. However, it should be noted that there are bound to be all kinds of uncontrolled and unidentified sources of variations, which render interpretation of results unpredictable. Nevertheless, comparative evaluation is a useful step towards explaining program outcomes.

Study Sample

In order to illustrate the methodological approach, labour education programs were chosen for investigation. This program area is seldom studied thoroughly, as the Hong Kong Government does not subvent any educational programs for factory workers. As different welfare agencies are experimenting various social work intervention strategies, they are appropriate for comparative evaluation.

As this study is exploratory in nature, only three welfare agencies will be selected for comparative evaluation. To ensure that the findings could reflect the highest variety in approaching, planning and implementing labour education programs, the selection of agencies will be made on the basis of distinctiveness of the agencies in organizational structure, work setting, and program design as well as intervention approaches (see Table 1).

The period chosen for evaluation will be limited to a duration of one year. To preserve the integrity of the selected agencies, the symbols, A, B & C will be used to replace the actual names of the selected agencies.

Agency A adopts a community service approach, which provides different kinds of community service to attract participation of factory workers in its labour education programs, which have no linkage with either trade union activities or labour disputes. Agency B adopts a community organizing approach, which stresses on the formation of labour groups to act on social issues that are related to the rights and welfare of factory workers. Agency C adopts a social action approach, which mobilizes workers in labour disputes to fight for their workers' rights and provide labour education programs to consolidate the campaign experiences in labour disputes.

Table 1. A brief overview of the general characteristicsof the three selected welfare agencies.

	Agency A	*Agency B*	*Agency C*
Agency goal	To provide community services	To provide social services for workers	To carry out an urban industrial mission
Sponsorship	United Methodist Church	Maryknoll Sisters	Ecumenical Church
Staff	1 Program Coordinator 2 Part-time Youth Workers 1 Clerk	1 Director 3 Group & Community Workers 1 Program Assistant	1 Director 1 Assistant Director 2 Workers 1 Part-time Worker
Work setting	Community Centre	Youth Centre	Office
Geographical setting	Resettlement estates & factory buildings (Kwai Chung)	Low-cost housing estates (Sau Mau Ping)	Commercial & financial centre (Tsimshatsui)
Types of services	Youth work Labour education Kindergarten Medical clinic Church Dress-making workshop	Youth work Library Community development Recreational services Industrial counselling Labour education	Evangelism Social researches Industrial relations Advisory service Labour education Case studies of industrial affairs
Intervention approach	Community service	Community organizing	Community action

Procedures of Assessing Effectiveness

To carry out an assessment of effectiveness on a program which is well-planned with clear and measurable objectives and fully recorded throughout its implementation, it may need no more than the following three simple steps (Weiss, 1972):

(1)   Translate the program objectives into measurable indicators.
(2)   Collect data on the indicators for those who participated (and those who did not) in the program.
(3)   Compare the data on participants (and the control group) with the criteria of successful achievement.

But to carry out a cross-program comparative evaluation study, a choice has to be made on a common program objective from out of the multiple objectives of various programs, and then an agreeable conception and measurable indicator of the chosen objective be developed. These must be well formulated before the steps stated above are to be implemented.

Choosing Common Objectives

To choose a common objective for comparative assessment, one needs to consider the following (Weiss, 1972):

(1)   feasibility of specifying the objective into a clear and measurable one;
(2)   relative importance of the objective;
(3)   compatibility of the objective with other stated objectives;
(4)   potential for utilization in decision-making; and
(5)   practicability in terms of time, effort, money and researchability.

Now let us look at the labour education program objectives of the three agencies:

Agency A

1. To encourage workers to be more aware of their rights and situations.
2. To facilitate workers to strive in an organized way for improving their welfare situations.
3. To develop their commitment and identity in the industrial field and enable them to perceive the value of their contribution to the economy.

Agency B

1. To help in raising workers' consciousness of the injustices in their working and living conditions.
2. To assist in the education and formation of workers' leaders and worker groups.
3. To encourage workers to protect their own human rights.

Agency C

1. To raise social consciousness about workers' own status and rights.
2. To promote solidarity of workers.
3. To help workers to fight for their social, political and economic benefits.

From the program objectives of the three agencies stated in the last chapter, the most suitable objective that is common to the three programs and, at the same time, satisfying the above criteria, is to "promote workers' consciousness of their rights". This objective is central to the concept of labour education, and is of great concern to most of the factory workers as well as the social work professionals.

Developing Measurable Indicators

To transform a program objective into a measurable indicator requires a specific observable conceptualization of the meaning of the objective. Such a conceptualization process is more than a linguistic exercise, as it determines the composition of the indicator.

According to the program staff of the three agencies, they all asserted that "consciousness of workers' rights" is something much more than the mere knowledge of existing labour laws and social reality, though they are fundamental to the development of consciousness. It also includes the capacity of assessing their given rights and social reality critically, and the readiness to exercise and/or fight for their given and warranted rights in society. Hence, the components of the concept "consciousness of rights" includes:

(1) Knowledge of existing labour laws.
(2) Capacity to assess labour and social affairs critically.
(3) Readiness to exercise the legal rights of workers in society.
(4) Readiness to fight for their deserved rights in society.

In view of the four components, the first two could be assessed by a mixed opinion measure, and the rest by the degree of the workers' actual participation in those activities. Such a design avoids the pitfalls of measuring either on attitudes, values, personality or knowledge, or on gross behavioural change. The former bases on a doubtful assumption that change in attitude or knowledge is a sufficient condition for behavioural change, and the latter is incomplete without the knowledge of intrapsychic change. As there is very few well constructed scales or indicators for measuring "consciousness", the investigator has to design some questions, tests and indicators to ascertain workers' knowledge, attitudes and behaviours. Such a design would inevitably involve the problems of reliability and validity. Hence, the result will be at most indicative and should not constitute a piece of conclusive assessment. And to enrich the understanding of the program's effectiveness, the opinions and the reflection of the program participants about the program will be collected to show their subjective feelings about the programs.

Knowledge and Opinion Measures

Since the purpose of this measure is to assess, firstly, the knowledge of the workers on labour laws and, secondly, their capacity in analyzing labour and societal affairs critically, the mixed measure is designed with the use of multiple choice questions on their knowledge of existing labour laws, the use of opinion questions on their ability to assess labour affairs, and the use of attitude statements (adopted from Radicalism-Conservation Scale (Robinson & Shaver, 1970) with modification to suit the local context) to assess their critical power over social reality.

The mixed measure could have been used to assess the different degrees of effectiveness of the three selected programs. But since the labour education programs are still at the initial stage of development in Hong Kong, it seems to be more fruitful to find out if the participants of the labour education courses show a better knowledge of labour laws and a higher capacity in assessing labour and social affairs critically than the non-participants. In order to cancel the effects of course learning and socialization process at the agency, the factory workers attending the ordinary evening schools and those joining agency programs other than labour education courses will be treated as two comparison groups. The results of the participant group will be compared with those of the non-participant groups by means of statistical tests (see Appendix 1).

Tables of Results

The findings reveal that participants of labour education courses of the three selected agencies show better knowledge of labour laws and higher capacity of critical assessment of labour and social affairs than non-participants, except for one category of evening school non-participants in relation to labour law knowledge. The results do indicate some sort of effectiveness of labour education courses in promoting workers' consciousness of their rights. However, the findings should be considered as exploratory and tentative, as special effort is needed to ascertain the validity and reliability of such a measure.

Behaviour Measure

To assess "readiness to exercise the legal rights of workers" and "ability to fight for their rights in society", it is hard to make direct observation on the behaviour of workers who might do it publicly or privately in their own surroundings. One of the appropriate measures one can use here is to assess the degree of the course participants' active pursuit of the labour education program and its related activities, in such matters as worker group functions, and reaction to issues on labour and society. Thus, some approximate data can be collected from the program staff to show the effectiveness of courses on their degree of participation in pursuing program activities, in joining workers' groups, and in reacting to social and labour issues.

The table shows clearly that within the year under investigation, Agency B has consistently the highest ratio of participating in pursuing program activities, reacting to issues and joining worker groups, while Agency C consistently has the highest number of participants in the mentioned form of participation. It is hard to judge which agency has a more effective program as there is a lack of comparable data with what was achieved the year before. Nevertheless, the table does give a clear description of what happens after attending courses in terms of participating in various forms of activities.

Treating the three programs as a whole, we see that of 48 courses, there is an average participation of 25 workers for every course. Of more than a thousand workers participated, the courses were effective in getting 1/5 to continue participating in the associated program activities, 1/14 to participate in reacting to social and labour issues, and 1/12 to join workers' group.

Table 2. Effectiveness of courses on course participants' behaviour.

| | *Agency* | | | |
Nature of Workers' Participation	*A*	*B*	*C*	*Total*
Number of courses held	8	10	30	48
Total no. of participants	80	200	900	1180
Ratio of participation in each course	1:10	1:20	1:30	1:25
Number of participants in pursuing program activities	20	60	150	230
Ratio of participation in pursuing program activities	1:4	1:3	1:6	1:5
Number of participants reacting to social and labour issues	8	25	50	83
Ratio of participation in reacting to social and labour issues	1:10	1:8	1:8	1:14
Number of participants joining workers groups	10	40	50	100
Ratio participation in joining worker groups	1:8	1:5	1:18	1:12

Another form of behaviour measure is to assess the number of worker groups developed as a result of the whole labour education programs. The data collected is shown in the following table:

Table 3. Nature of workers' group developed in the programs.

Nature of Workers' Groups	*Agency A*	*Agency B*	*Agency C*
1. Steering Group	Workers Steering Committee*	Youth Governing Board*	Executive Committee
2. Education Group	Education Group*	Young Workers Group	Course Management Group
3. Cultural Group	Drama Club* Cultural Group*	Friendship Club	—
4. Publication Group	Experimental Writer*	Newsletter Group*	—
5. Service Group	—	Workers Service Group* Library Volunteers Group*	Secretariat* Publicity Group*
6. Recreation Group	Youth Group*	Hau Ching Group	Activity Group*
7. Action Group	—	—	Social Survey Group* Labour Rights Group*
8. Production Group	—	Arts and Crafts Production Cooperative*	—
Total no. of groups	6	7	7
*No. of groups developed within the year of investigation	6	5	6
No. of workers involved	40	70	60
Average Group Size	7	12	10

There is more or less a similar number of groups developed within the year of investigation, but Agency B and Agency C have a relatively larger average group size than that of Agency A. Agency B outpaces the other two agencies in having a production group whereas Agency C is better in forming two action groups. Relatively speaking, Agency A is weak in developing service, action and production type of grouping, while Agency B and C are weak in action, cultural and publication groups respectively. On the whole, the three agencies are able to establish five to six groups of workers with an average membership of 10.

Apart from performing the usual group functions, some of these workers' groups such as steering groups, education groups, publication groups, action groups and production group, are found to pursue a clear objective of promoting workers' consciousness. And they work towards these objectives through planning and coordinating their own programs, organizing their own courses, expressing their viewpoints in bulletins, reacting together to issues and experimenting collective devise of production. The formation of these groups strongly demonstrates the effectiveness of the programs in getting the workers to participate and to strive for their rights in society.

In the Words of Workers

The workers who had joined the program have the following feelings about their participation in labour education programs:

> "We feel that through preparing and participating in the work and activities, we gained much practical knowledge. In addition, both new and old members are able to come to know each other better."
> "From our contact with other young workers, we have learnt that most young workers have only a primary education. If they are aware of their educational needs and if their working conditions allow, many could have studied in school."

"Participation in group has taught us that the young workers need to liberate themselves from their too hectic and too tense style of living. We need to develop ourselves both mentally and physically, and in this way, continue to grow."
"Young workers are in a better position to participate in the centre's work of making policy, planning, organizing and supervision. In the future, through participation, we'll have greater opportunities to exhibit our leadership qualities."

The picture painted by these participants towards the program effect would have been even more complete if the viewpoints of the program dropouts have been solicited.

A Recapitulation of Program Effectiveness

There is a slight indication that the participants of the labour education courses conducted by the selected agencies have show a better knowledge of labour laws and possessed a more critical capacity to assess labour and social affairs than those who have just joined and participated in the same agencies for other functions or attended evening school. But which agency program produced the best effect still awaits future study.

In terms of the program effect on readiness to exercise and to fight for workers' rights, Agencies B and C seemed to have fared slightly better than Agency A, whose program at the year chosen for study was in its first year of development. On the whole, all three agencies were able to get from the course participants a similar degree of workers' participation and group development which helps promote workers' consciousness. And in the words of participants, they did appreciate and value the opportunity to learn, to express, to act and to grow.

Reflections on Evaluation Issues

Many issues arose during the course of the comparative evaluation study. It is important that self-reflection be made and that various issues be identified and discussed.

Issue 1 Program requirement for evaluation

To start an evaluation exercise, one must be sure that the program is well planned with concrete objectives and clear expectation of effects. Without such a prerequisite, one would not be able to do the evaluation. For instance, a program with the following planning requirements could facilitate evaluation exercises:

a. Target group: What specific group of people is the program addressed to? And what are their needs to be met?
b. Content of objective: What changes in observable and measurable terms, and in what nature, be it information, opinions, attitudes or behaviour, is the program intended to produce effects?
c. Emergence of effect: How quickly is the program intended to produce effects?
d. Magnitude of effect: How large is an effect expected?
e. Stability of effect: How long are the effects produced by the program intended to last?
f. Unintended consequences: What are the possible side effects of the program?

It seems essential social workers be given training so as to be able to plan programs in these dimensions. Or else, it would be difficult to conduct a proper evaluation.

Issue 2 Program stage for evaluation

A program has different stages of development. To make evaluation more relevant and responsive to program development, one needs to consider what Tripodi (1978) proposed as "Differential Evaluation". The process of differential evaluation involves delineating evaluation objectives that are appropriate to specific stages of program development and choosing evaluation strategies pertinent to these objectives. In short, differential evaluation should involve the following (see Tripodi, 1978; p. 107):

1. Specification of long-range and immediate operating goals and the means to accomplish these goals.
2. Determination of the current stage of program development and collection of information about problem in attaining goals of former or subsequent stages.
3. Delineation of a hierarchy of program objectives in terms of their importance to the program.
4. Formulation of evaluation objectives relevant to important program objectives for the current stage of program development.
5. Selection of evaluation strategies that will provide information pertaining to evaluation objectives, within time and cost constraints of the program.
6. Review of information retrieved through evaluation and translation into decisions about future program planning.

Issue 3 Multiple problem perspective for evaluation

It is important to note that a person seeking service may have multiple problems. One type of service may not be sufficient to tackle the complicated problem. For example a teen-age girl who becomes pregnant may need as many as 10 services including parental medical care, prenatal education, obstetrical care, vocational education, job placement, day, care etc. Hence, a multiple perspective on program evaluation will be helpful:

> "Although a highly specialized treatment may be judged 'effective' by the provider it may be judged relatively inadequate by the client if there is no system of related treatments or services to help with the interrelated cluster of problems ... Evaluation must address the issues implicit in the single-input fallacy — the belief that a single service or treatment, in isolation of others, will be sufficient to restore a multiproblemed individual to an effective level of overall functioning" (Attkisson & Broskowski, 1978; p. 8).

It seems that both practitioners and evaluators must bear in mind the importance of multiple problem perspective and multiple intervention approach.

Issue 4 Evaluation of effectiveness

There is a general belief that the evaluator, by means of scientific research, can tell whether a program is effective or not. In reality, it is not the case. An evaluator can at best find out the degree of effectiveness in relation to certain criteria. But does that "degree" of effectiveness constitute an "effective" program remains a value judgement. As pointed out in the Encyclopaedia of Social Sciences, (Wright, 1968):

> "... the question of just how much effectiveness constitute[s] success and justifies the effort or the program is unanswerable by scientific research. It remains a matter of judgement on the part of the program sponsors, administrators, critics, or others and the benefits must somehow be balanced against the cost involved.
>
> The problem is complicated further by the fact that most action programs have multiple goals, each of which may be achieved with varying degrees of success over time and among different subgroups of participants in the programs".

Hence, the question we need to consider is, "Who is to make the judgement on effectiveness?" Do the frontline practitioners and the service consumers have a say in the decision process?

Summary

The word "evaluation" sounds threatening. Any negative findings in an evaluation report would mean degrading or even the scrapping of a program. Hence, it is not surprising that many people, including professionals, are psychologically resistant to any kind of evaluation. However, in describing the conduct and the process of this comparative evaluation of three labour education programs, it is hoped that a lot of unnecessary fear could be demystified. It is evident that a systematic evaluation would definitely improve our understanding of what works and what does not. An additional message seems to tell us that even a social work program that is not well established, such as labour education, can be evaluated in a simple manner, and practitioners themselves are equally capable of conducting self-evaluation. Perhaps, both from an administrative and professional points of view, we can still make a lot of sense from the concluding remarks of the 1975 Seminar on Evaluation convened by the Social Welfare Department (1976) of the Hong Kong Government:

1. Evaluation is necessary to ensure both the value for money and that agency services develop in response to changing community needs.
2. In future, evaluation should look at an area of service as a whole, rather than at individual agencies.
3. Detail planning is a necessary prerequisite to evaluation.
4. Agencies should conduct self-evaluation on a continuing basis.
5. Before embarking on any new evaluation exercise, the Social Welfare Department (SWD) and Hong Kong Council of Social Service (HKCSS) should consult with agencies on the objectives of evaluation, methods and procedures, and on possible consequences of evaluation.
6. In any future evaluation, the views of service recipients should be taken into consideration whenever possible.
7. Independent experts should be involved in evaluation.

Surely, it is in the interest of the professionals, the administrators, the finding body, the state and above all, the service users, to pursue quality evaluation of social work services.

References

Attkisson & Broskowski (1978) "Evaluation and the emerging human service concept" in *Evaluation of Human Service Program*, Academic Press.
Hong Kong Government (1991) *Social Welfare into the 1990s and Beyond*. The White Paper on Social Welfare.

Mok, H. (1987) "Citizen participation in social welfare planning: A case study of Hong Kong from 1973 to 1986" Unpublished Ph.D. Thesis. Department of Social Policy and Administration, London School of Economics. Chapter 7.

______, (1982) "Evaluation and outreaching social work" reprinted in *Outreach*, Writers' Cooperative, 1990, pp. 235–242.

Robinson, J & P. Shaver (1970) *Measures of Social Psychological Attitudes*. Survey Research Center, p. 392.

Social Welfare Department (1994) *Report on Review of Children and Youth Centre Services*. Working Party on Review of Children and Youth Centre Services, April 1994.

______, (1976) *Seminar Proceedings on Evaluation*, Hong Kong Government, January, 1975.

Suchman, E.A. (1967) *Evaluation Research*. N.Y.: Russell Sage Foundation.

Tripodi *et al.* (1978) *Differential Social Program Evaluation*. Peacock Publisher, U.S.A.

Weiss, C. (1972) *Evaluation Research: Method of Assessing Program Effectiveness*. Prentice Hall.

Wright, C. (1968) "Evaluation research" in *Encyclopaedia of Social Sciences*, Vol. 5.

Appendix 1

Knowledge and Opinion Measures

Objective

To test if the participants of the Labour Education programs of the selected agencies have a better knowledge of the existing labour legislations and better capacity in analyzing labour and social affairs more critically than the non-participating workers.

Study Design

Since the participants received the education at the agencies, the agency members and evening school workers' students will be taken as the control group for cancelling the effects of course learning and socialization process at the agency. Therefore, 3 groups of workers are used in the study. They are:

Group 1   Participants of Labour Education Courses
Group 2   Agency members not participating in the Courses
Group 3   Evening school students not participating in the Courses

The results of the participant group will be compared with those of the non-participant groups by means of a statistical test.

Measurements

Type A   **General Knowledge**: 7 multiple choice questions were set on the existing labour laws to assess their knowledge.

Type B   **Opinion Questions**: 8 questions were set on labour affairs to asses the capacity to analyze labour affairs critically.

Type C   **Attitude Statements**: 15 attitude statements were set on hypothetical social situations to assess the capacity to analyze social affairs critically.

Scoring System

Type A   1 point for each correct answer.
Type B   Progressive scores from 1 to 5 in accordance with the degree of the critical nature of the answers pre-set by the design.
Type C   The Lickert 7-point scale scoring is used.

Statistical Test

One-tail Z test is used for comparing two means with the 2 control samples respectively.

Study Sample

Restricted to manual workers over 14 years of age. The agency staff were responsible for distributing the survey forms to Groups 1 and 2. Two classes of students of an average evening school participated in the survey through the help of a school teacher.

Sample Size

Not less than 30 respondents for each Group.

Part II
Cases Studies on Social Services Administration in Local Context

4

Adaptation of an Organization to the Environment and Its Implication to Its Internal Structure: A Case Analysis of the Hong Kong Council of Social Service before Restructuring

SEZTO Wai Chu, Rachel

Introduction

The Hong Kong Council of Social Service (hereafter called the HKCSS) is the sole social service organization which co-ordinates welfare services operated by non-governmental organizations (hereafter called NGOs) in Hong Kong and represents NGOs in the negotiation with the Government in areas of policy formulation and social welfare development. Its unique role and subsequent lack of competition easily lead to the perception that its adaptation, if necessary, is a much simpler task when compared with that of other social service organizations.

Though monopoly may pave a smoother way for existence, the HKCSS' survival and effective functioning in response to current external changes require in-depth examination of the environment, awareness of the threat posed to the agency, and design of adaptation strategies correspondingly.

Being the sole co-ordinating body of NGOs in Hong Kong, the HKCSS does have special consideration for and linkage with the environment which constitutes less of a threat to other NGOs. Also, the relative small proportion of direct service it engages in deprives it of the attention of sponsors, hence access to outside resources is limited.

Faced with this unique environment, adaptation strategies to be adopted by the HKCSS are inevitably devised from both its own interpretation of external threats and assessment of its internal strength.

In the process of reviewing the HKCSS' internal environment, its structure is picked up as the focal point of examination and analysis. The choice of structure as an element of linking the organization's adaptation to the environment stems from the close interrelationship among these three elements, which is already proven by the abundant valuable literature accumulated through decades, for example, those elaborated by P. Lawrence & J. Lorsch.

Most importantly, in the face of the increasing source of turbulence from the macro-system, where effective exertion of control of influence presents a long battle to fight, adaptation through improving the organization's structure is comparatively easier to be maneuvered, and is also a pre-requisite if goals on the macro-level are to be developed and pursued in the long-run.

It is against this background that this research project starts, with the aim to answer the questions below.

Questions to be Answered in this Study

- What is the implication of the HKCSS' environment and its adaptation measures to its structure?
- What insight can be gained in the analysis so as to shed light on the formulation of future adaptation strategies?

Limitation

This study inevitably examines a complex issue in a narrow perspective. Other factors, which are equally critical in affecting an organization's adaptation, such as management leadership and culture, will not be taken into account in this research project. However, some of the traits of these factors can be implicitly reflected when the structure of the organization is analyzed.

Time Frame

Finally, this project research will adopt a time frame which started from January 1990, the year in which the preparation of the White Paper of "Social Welfare into the 1990s and Beyond" commenced, until the end of the 1994 calendar year. Though environmental changes are continuously taking place and it is impossible to set a clear cut-off date, the latest issue of the White Paper on social welfare is nevertheless the most remarkable cornerstone for inauguration.

Theoretical Perspectives

There are many theories or approaches developed to account for the relationship between the environment and the organization. In this research project, an integration of the contingency theory into the political-economy approach will be adopted as a framework for analyzing the environment and the adaptation strategies.

The choice of using a combination of these two approaches mainly originates from their common characteristics in focusing on the interaction between the environment and the organization's internal structure. In addition, the differences are essentially complimentary.

From the viewpoint of the contingency theory, there should be congruence between the internal structure of an organization and the environment. The more homogeneous and stable the environment is, the less differentiated but more standardized the internal structure is, and vice versa. Though offering a quite straight-forward inference from the external environment to internal structure, the contingency theory pays little regard concerning the difference among organizations, that is, organizations facing the same environment may not have the same level of resources.

This limitation can be supplemented by the political-economy approach which stresses that the two resources that an organization should garner in response to the changing environment are legitimacy and power (i.e., the political resources) as well as production resources (i.e. economic resources). The availability and accessibility of these resources greatly affect how the organization shapes its internal structure to adapt to the environment.

Hence, in the following parts, observation on environmental changes will be highlighted and their implications to the HKCSS in the following dimensions will be analyzed:

- Heterogeneity
- Instability
- Endangered legitimacy and decline of power
- Shrinkage of resources

Analysis of Environment & Its Implication to the HKCSS

Heterogeneity

Arising New Pattern of Service Delivery

Recently, quite a number of new initiatives of service delivery pattern have been promoted or finally implemented by the Social Welfare Department. Here are some examples: restructuring of group work units in the community centres into family activity resource centre, implementation of the concept of integration through the establishment of integrated teams of children and youth services, the transfer of intermediate treatment from the United Kingdom to Hong Kong as the community support service scheme for young people with minor offences, etc.

At the same time, there is also a comparable trend in the NGOs. There is a growing number of non-subvented service, operated either by newly-established agencies or existing agencies which are already delivering other subvented services. These include the use of mediation in settling family dispute as an alternative of the traditional family service, provision of temporary residential service for young people, etc. They are usually operating in a relatively small scale to fill the gap between existing subvented services.

Regardless of their origins from the Government's conscious effort on value for money or the spirit of voluntary agency, these varieties of service types constitute an environment of greater heterogeneity for the HKCSS to tackle.

The existing structure of the HKCSS' various Divisions mainly builds on a basis of individual responsibility of a particular Committee on a specific kind of service. The Management Committee of the Division should be responsible for overseeing the overall issues pertaining to their specific target groups, such as the elderly or the family and they may also easily get pre-occupied with the development of existing services.

As one of the characteristics of NGOs is to pilot new initiatives, the HKCSS' orientation and ability in fostering this spirit and supporting NGOs gearing towards this direction are essential. However, the existing co-ordinating mechanism may limit the capacity of the HKCSS to accommodate this homogeneous environment and also hinders its work in promoting the pioneering spirit of NGOs.

Diversification of Stakeholders

The stakeholders of the HKCSS include the Government, who provides it with both the majority of financial resources and the recognized role in co-ordinating the social services operated by the NGOs and the member agencies, which delegate it with the power of collective representation of their interests in pursuing issues related to the development of social service. While the turbulent environment arising from the Government will be tackled in the next part, the one created by the member agencies will be the focus of this part.

Since 1991, with the publication of the White Paper "Social Welfare into the 1990s and Beyond" which advocates the spirit of support network, there has been an evident trend of growing variety of social service agencies which are not operating mainstream subvented service joining the HKCSS as member agencies. These agencies are self-help organizations of disadvantaged groups, such as parents of handicapped children, patients with chronic illness, or voluntary groups such as Hong Kong Aircraft Engineering Co., Veterans Club Ltd., and agencies operating non-subvented service, like Land of Virtue Company Limited.

This diversification in the nature of stakeholders poses another aspect of heterogeneity to HKCSS. Being an organization composed by member agencies, the fulfillment of members' expectations and having different expectations balanced are of critical importance. However, this growing diversity of the nature of member agencies may either paralyse the organization as they are representing different interests which may be in conflict in some issues, or lead to passive participation of non-mainstream member agencies whose interests may be scarified or overlooked by major stakeholders.

In negotiating with the Government as a collective representation of NGOs, the HKCSS relies a lot on the support and consensus from its member agencies as its base of power. However, if it fails to secure their overall support or consensus, the growth in the number of member agencies will only become an obstacle.

Instability

The development of welfare service of Hong Kong is always heavily affected by the economic situation, which in turn hinges on the complex dynamics of capitalists' interests, political considerations and international influence. These factors, not to mention their combination, are in fact far from the prediction and control of the HKCSS.

Such instability is further enhanced by the great investment in the new airport and the subsequent unresolved lengthy conflict between the British and PRC Governments. In spite of the investment of 60 billion HK dollars into the welfare sector as claimed by the Address made by the Governor in October 1994, a large part of the money was used only in the fulfillment of delayed promises all geared towards remedial service. The minimal state intervention on welfare together with the financial burden envisaged inevitably has led to declining commitment to welfare sector. All kinds of measures for value for money, in the name of cost-effectiveness, especially in developmental and preventive services, will follow.

In addition, with the entrance into the post-transitional stage, the growing intervention from the PRC Government is manifesting and becoming obvious. The speech made by Mr. Zhou Nan, Director of Xinhua News Agency, Hong Kong Branch, in late 1994 might reflect the remedial orientation of the PRC Government towards social welfare, and hinted on a pessimistic road ahead for welfare services in Hong Kong.

For the HKCSS, the unstable environment created by the Government not only heralds an era of reducing financial resources for both herself and the whole welfare sector, but the possible weakening of the partnership relationship between NGOs and the Government also foretells the diminishing of the consultative role of the HKCSS in welfare issues.

Endangered Legitimacy

Recognition from the Government

As previously mentioned, the role of the HKCSS in co-ordinating and representing the view of NGOs operating social service is recognized by the Government, and only with such a granted legitimacy can the organization function effectively.

However, from a few incidents of formulating important policy taking place these years, there seems to be a trend that the legitimate role of the HKCSS in representing the NGOs' views is only recognized when the outcome is obviously in line with the expectation of the Government. Otherwise, if the represented view is predicted to be in conflict with the Government's wish or to add complexity to the task, the legitimate role of the HKCSS will be overlooked, or even rejected when requested.

In some joint forums chaired by the Government, HKCSS staff has been invited to attend on personal capacity. This implies that he/she had neither the need to consult the views of member agencies concerning the discussion items nor the right to disclose confidential information discussed in the forum. Moreover, for issues that have implications on the overall development or policy of the service, the Government did directly contact individual agencies and try to get their consent one by one instead of going through the normal and well-recognized channel of the HKCSS.

In addition to the overwhelming dependency of the HKCSS financial resources on the Government, the fact that a great portion of services operated by NGOs is funded by the Government sheds light on the crisis that once the HKCSS is deprived of its legitimate role by the Government, the support from the member agencies will be lowered since most of the time the bargaining target of the NGOs is the Government.

Declining Political Power

There was a time when the HKCSS was blacklisted by the Government as a pressure group that urged too much for better welfare and livelihood of the citizens. The ability to mobilize the support and response from its member agencies has inevitably posed a threat to the Government, and this also became a political power of the HKCSS in negotiating with the Government. However, with the rise of both a representative Government and the establishment of various political parties, the fight for better welfare is found in the political agenda of every candidate for councilor. This role of the HKCSS as an advocacy group together with its influential political power in bargaining with the Government are no more unique.

At the same time, having served as a Legislative Councilor for ten years, the Director of the HKCSS has recently announced his stepping down from the political stage in the 1995 election. His dual role in the past years has in fact facilitated the functioning of the HKCSS in various aspects, such as the access to first-hand information about the Government's orientation on certain welfare issues, the schedule of policy formulation, his personal linkage with the high officials of the Government and his personal influence on other Legislative Councilors on welfare issues The delinking of these roles weakens both the HKCSS' political power as well as its influence on the Government and its strength in performing the watchdog on welfare issues.

These two factors contribute to the overall decline of political power of the HKCSS. Serving as a bridge between the Government and the NGOs, such diminishing influential position will pose difficulties to future work and also worsen the ongoing shrinkage of resources.

Shrinkage of Resources

Scarcity of resources has always been a common environment faced by nonprofit-making organizations. In the context of the HKCSS in recent years, we shall take the following types of resources into consideration.

Financial Resources

Though the financial resources provided by the Government has shown a rise of 37.5% from 1991 to 1994, its actual proportion in the total income of the HKCSS shows a decline (see Table 1).

Table 1. Percentage of government subvention in HKCSS total income 1990–94.

Year	Percentage (%)
90–91	81.52
91–92	81.64
92–93	79.93
93–94	79.54

Personnel

Manpower resources in the HKCSS not only serve to maintain the daily ongoing function of the organization, but are also valuable resources as they are equipped with knowledge of the history of the development of various services, issues discussed, and personal linkage with member agencies. For the past three years, the manpower turnover for professional staff is around 2.3, and the situation is worse in the Development Team (see Table 2). Though it is difficult to comment on whether or not such a turnover rate is high, the need to maintain and develop staff as resources and an asset to the organization are essential especially in the face of another serious brain drain when approaching 1997.

Table 2. Turnover of professional staff of HKCSS 1990–94.

	No. of Professional Posts existed all through the years	*No. of persons occupying these posts*	*Turnover rate*
Agency Service Team	14	30	2.1
Development Team	21	52	2.5
Overall	35	82	2.3

Information

The importance of updated information about both current social issues and service development of member agencies is undeniable for the HKCSS to perform effectively its co-ordinating role, especially in this period of time when much new social needs as well as new initiatives attempted by the NGOs arise. In spite of its critical importance, the input, processing, storage and retrieval of information lack both systematic planning and operation. Fragmented and piecemeal information is kept by different units and the leave of any person-in-charge definitely leads to problems of information inaccessibility.

The depreciation and lack of consciousness to develop these production resources entrench the HKCSS into an unfavourable position in both performing its coordinating role and also a re-examination of its positioning.

The above analysis from both the perspectives of the organization's environment and the resources it can master brings out the vicious cycle that the HKCSS is going through. The ongoing insufficiency of resources reduces its ability to cope with the turbulent and unstable environment. The ineffectiveness of the organization in performing its roles further weakens its incentives to attract resources, and hence again lowers the availability of resources (see Fig. 1).

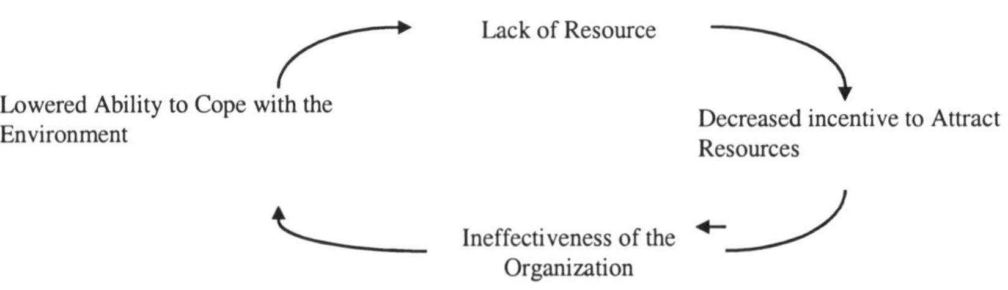

Fig. 1

Adaptation Measures Taken

In the face of the turbulent and unstable environment outlined above, the HKCSS is not unaware of the needs of adaptation. Therefore, in the past four years under review, quite a lot of new attempts have been tried out possibly with the aim of equipping the organization with a more responsive attribute as well as enhancing its effectiveness. These attempts are now grouped into two categories, namely, maximization of resources and a venture into new domains, and elaborated below.

Maximization of Resources

Political and economic resources are the two most critical resources for an organization to survive. The previous section has already provided a picture of a decline of these two resources in the HKCSS. In tackling the shrinkage of various types of resources, the following measures have been put into practice.

Economic Resources

Bidding of New Project to Supplement Existing Insufficiency

A post of Senior Project Officer has been created to be responsible for providing drug-abuse information and in-service training for staff in the welfare sector. Besides, the Officer will also be responsible for overseeing issues like implementation of the three-year plans of the HKCSS, town planning and education. However, since this post was only supported by a part-time secretary and its work has relatively little linkage with other components, the full functioning was highly limited. In 1993, with the increase in social concern about HIV and AIDS, the Government pumped resources in public education about AIDS. By that time, conscious of both its roles in providing training on AIDS for social welfare personnel and the resources that can be brought in, an AIDS Project under the Senior Project Officer was established in the HKCSS with the funding support from the AIDS Trust Fund. The original team has expanded to a team with three professional staff and three clerical staff, and also equipped with a comprehensive set of updated office equipment, which can hardly be found in other components. Though the original designated use of this funding resources was for the promotion of proper attitudes towards AIDS and provide training for social welfare staff, they are in fact flexibly deployed to assist the Senior Project Officer in carrying out the other domains of work he is responsible for, such as drug abuse. This flexible utilization of resources from a new project is a means to enlarge the financial resources.

Membership Drive

Membership does not only provide the base of power and the representativeness of the HKCSS, but membership fee is also a source of financial resources. Recognizing these multiple importance, the HKCSS re-named the post of Development Secretary as Development Executive in 1992/93. The change of title aims at conveying a more appealing image of the person in-charge of this task to potential donors as well as new agencies, and therefore implying that the post-holder is expected to undertake a more energetic move in boosting up the size of membership and exploring new sponsoring bodies to support member agencies' projects requiring funds.

Reviewing the figures of membership in these years, the number of full member has stuck to 158 since 1990–91 and it was only in 1993/94 that it rose to 165, and also in the same year, the number of associate members ultimately broke the line of 50 with a total of 53 at the end of May 1994. However, with a further investigation into membership fee as an income of the HKCSS, it is strangely found that the amount fluctuated and drops were found in 1991, 1993, and 1994 (see Tables 3 & 4).

Without bringing in any substantial financial resources, the rise of membership can only be regarded as an asset if it can provide other types of resources to the HKCSS, for example, the support in backing up the HKCSS to bargain with the Government concerning development of social welfare policy, or bringing in new stimulation to service delivery models. However, as previously elaborated, the existing co-ordinating forum provides limited space for these newly member agencies to participate as most of them are not providing mainstream subvented service.

Table 3. HKCSS membership 1990–94.

Year	Full Member	Associate Member	Total
90–91	158	48	206
91–92	158	50	208
92–93	158	49	207
93–94	165	53	218

Table 4. Percentage of income generated through membership fee in the in HKCSS total income 1990–94

Year	Percentage (%)
90–91	1.84
91–92	2.14
92–93	1.85
93–94	1.59

Exploration of Outside Funding Resources

Besides relying on the major funding sources, like the subvention from the Government, Community Chest and membership fee, it is found that the HKCSS is paying much effort to explore outside funding resources in such ways as hiring additional contract staff either to take up specific task originally performed by permanent staff or to be responsible for short-term special projects which are believed to facilitate the manifestation of the image of the organization to the public, such as the organization of Expo 2000 in 1993, the International Day of Disabled Person, etc. The expansion of staff team thus resulted definitely helps alleviate the ever-increasing workload of the permanent staff.

Political Resources

Liaison with Political Parties and Formation of Alliance

Though it was in November 1994 that the Director of the HKCSS announced his stepping down from the political stage in 1995, there have been conscious moves taken by the HKCSS to develop linkage with political parties and individual councilors in order to solicit their support in pursuing welfare issues in the past few years instead of solely relying on the Director. Examples include the welfare cut in 1991, the urge for unification of pre-education service in 1994, the advocacy work in counteracting public discrimination against the establishment of both a day activity centre for the ex-mentally ill in Laguna City and the Parents Resource Centre for Down Syndrome Children in Tung Tau Estate in 1993, etc. Moreover, to facilitate staff understanding and easy reference on the platform and the positions of different political parties on social issues, a Resource File on Political Parties has been compiled.

To compensate for the foreseeable decline of political influence, close co-operation with the Hong Kong Social Workers Association and the Hong Kong Social Workers' General Union has been initiated. In the very early stage, an *ad hoc* basis co-operation was found among the three bodies. However, since 1993, formal and regular meetings were held to explore areas for co-operation. The formation of a relationship like an alliance among these three bodies definitely empowers each other.

Establishing Macro-level Influence

The limitation created by the pre-occupation with specific service in the co-ordination mechanism of the HKCSS has already been explained. To compensate for such a confined domain and to respond to the need for a more comprehensive view on welfare issues arising from the dazzling changes in the society, a new forum called the Committee on Social Welfare Development was formed in August 1993 to be responsible for giving advice on the overall direction of social welfare development. As this Committee has only been formed for a year with only five meetings held, its actualization of the ambitious aim and the ability to serve as a recognized corresponding mechanism in giving advice to the Government and providing direction to other welfare services are still to be seen.

When the sovereignty of the Hong Kong was resumed by the PRC Government in 1997, it was predicted that the previous advantage of the HKCSS in linking up with international bodies as a British colony might reduce, hence the HKCSS has also been devoting much effort in consolidating its international status and its linkage with the relevant government departments of the PRC. The series of international conferences it held and the frequent exchange activities with the PRC Government are all valid evidence of the HKCSS's effort in these directions. The overwhelming coverage on international events in the Chairman's Remarks in the Annual Report of the HKCSS in 1993/94 can substantiate this observation.

Adventure into New Domains

Apart from exploration and accumulation of resources, the HKCSS is also answering the challenge posed by the environment through its ventures into new domains. As a co-ordinating body of the NGOs which operate social service, the HKCSS also looks into or creates areas for development still untouched in the field of social welfare. This enlargement of task domain not only brings in new financial resources, but also consolidates the necessity of the existence of the organization since it is the only organization in Hong Kong which takes up such a task and its undertaking occupies such a great proportion in the whole field that replacement is difficult. In times of diminishing legitimacy of its co-ordinating roles, exploration of new areas is an alternative.

AIDS Project

The details of this Project has already been stated. Besides providing an opportunity to strengthen the originally insufficient resources, this Project also provides a new and unique area of domain for training of staff members about AIDS. Moreover, the HKCSS has its uniqueness and advantages in doing this in view of its established linkage with the social service agencies through its existing network. For example, the provision of training and education for home helpers are made more ready when their resistance was first identified through its Service Committee.

Hotline Service

In the HKCSS Annual General Meeting in 1992, the hotline service was inaugurated by the Governor and this heralded the commencement of another area of work of the HKCSS. This hotline provides enquirers with information of social service in Hong Kong and enquirers will be referred to the appropriate organization of assistance when they are in need. In addition, it also provides the public with information in making wise decisions on their donations.

For example, for enquiries about service provision in a specific district, a working mother will make use of the hotline to enquire the nearest after-school care service for her child. Thus the need for updated information of service units in different districts and a clear understanding of the nature and content of different services are necessary since the enquirer may only be able to spell out his/her need but not the exact service that is required.

Employee Retraining Programme

Employment Service is the only unit of the HKCSS that provides direct service to clients. The target clients of the Employment Service are those with unfavourable background and those experiencing difficulties in securing a job. They may be the ex-mentally ill, young persons discharged from special schools, boys' homes or girls' homes, etc.

In February 1994, with the sponsorship of the Employees Retraining Board of the Government, the Employment Service started the project of Employee Retraining Programme. Within a month since its inauguration, six orientation courses have been organized and till the end of the fiscal year of 1994, there were still 400 applicants waiting for enrollment. Additional staff members are employed and part of the existing staff in the Employment Service are redeployed for the implementation of the Project.

Taking up of Post in International Forum

The HKCSS has all along been active in participating in international events concerning social welfare, and this is held responsible mainly by the International and Regional Affairs Department. Since late 1994, this internationalization has further been strengthened by the election of the Assistant Director (Development) of the HKCSS as the Vice-chairman of the International Conference on Social Welfare (ICSW). This may signal a period of greater involvement in international social affairs, and in order to guarantee smooth functioning of this post, a grant was provided by the ICSW for the establishment of the Office of Vice-President within the HKCSS.

Highlight of HKCSS' Structure

Before analysing how the above adaptive measures affect the structure of the HKCSS, it is necessary to briefly highlight its existing structure and the characteristics as detailed below.

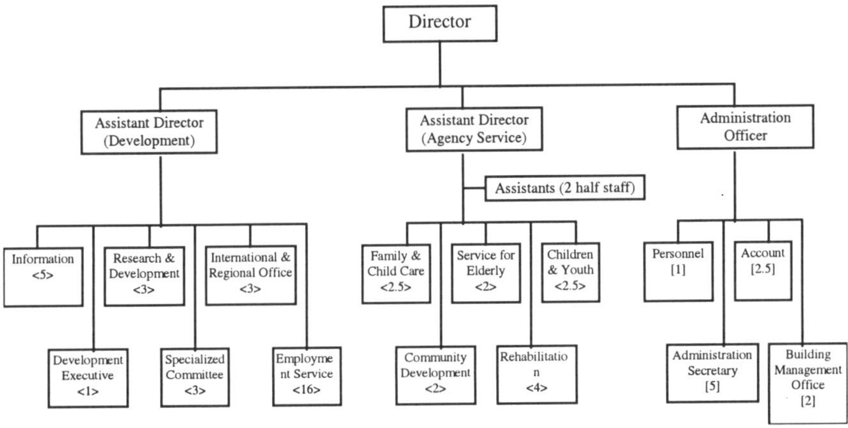

<> No. of professional staff

[ ] No. of staff

Fig. 2 Organization chart (as at the end of December 1994).

Characteristics of HKCSS' Structure

In analysing the characteristics of the HKCSS's structure, the framework proposed by Indick & Berrien will be adopted, while the four composing structures raised will be elaborated below, and the final one, which is the relationship with the environment, will be elaborated in depth in the next part.

Authority Structure

The line of authority in the HKCSS is more than what the above organization chart can show. Besides being accountable to their immediate supervisor, the staff of the HKCSS are also held accountable to the Committees and Working Groups to which the particular staff is responsible. For example, the work of the service Divisions is guided by the correponding Management Committee in addition to the Assistant Director (Agency Service). These Management Committees formulate the year plan of the Divisions and promote co-ordination and planning as well as consultation of the respective issues within the domain of the Divisions.

In most cases, the staff are to take action according to the decisions made by their governing Committee delegated by their immediate supervisors, except in critical issues concerning major recommendations in policy of operation. For these latter cases, advice and direction from the immediate supervisors are usually sought before putting the issue onto the meeting table. Nevertheless, there are also some incidents that decisions on minor issues made by the Working Group or Committee are rejected by the supervisor of the responsible staff. Creating a dilemma for the staff in deciding whose decision to act upon.

Communication Structure

The communication and interaction between units of different teams are relatively formal and standardized when compared with those within the same team. Normalization is more obvious when the message to be conveyed relates to feedback or aims at soliciting the views of members of another unit.

Nevertheless, horizontal communication between units, both inter-team and intra-team, is dominant. Generally speaking, it is very common for the units to initiate dialogue with or request information from other units. Appeal to liaison between supervisors is rarely necessary.

Specification of Roles and Tasks

The roles and tasks are clear between different units. For the seven units of the Development Team, each of them is an expert in a specific area of work such that seldom can other units replace each other's function. On the other hand, though the five Divisions of Agency service team are responsible for their respective service, the growing number of issues involving concerted services leads to the occurrence of incidents that it is difficult to decide which Division is to be held solely responsible. For example, the extension of the United Nation's Convention of the Rights of Child to Hong Kong involves both the Family Service and Child Care Division and the Children and Youth Division to a great extent.

Reward Structure

The formal reward structure of the HKCSS is weak in that both reinforcement of good performance and disciplinary action are difficult to be found. Only long-service awards for staff working continuously for ten years are granted. Since 1992, commendation letters are conferred to staff whose performance is outstanding by their supervisors' assessment in annual appraisals.

On the other hand, due to the relatively close relationship among staff, especially below the level of directorate grade, an informal reward structure is more commonly found. However, this varies greatly from unit to unit due to different management styles of the persons-in-charge.

Implications of Adaptive Measures on Structure

Growing Complexity of Organization & Inadequacy of Integrative Device

As stated in the previous part, specification of roles and differentiation of tasks within the HKCSS are already generally high. Some of the adaptive measures which aim at venturing into new domains are in fact adding more roles to the HKCSS or breaking existing roles into more details. For example, the operation of hotline to help enquirers make a wise decision in donation is a brand new area that none of the units within the HKCSS has even attempted. However, the task of disseminating information related to service provision has been previously unclearly shared by the Information Department and the respective service Divisions.

Both the taking up of new roles and the breaking down of existing roles are adding complexities to the organization structure. As the effective performance of the roles of each unit is quite dependent on the complementary function of other units, it is necessary for the staff to gain a full understanding of the roles of each other and hence adjust his/her own work to suit the others. This may require an understanding of acquisition of necessary information and the matching of time schedules of work in case both units are serving similar, if not the same, group of member agencies.

In this highly inter-dependent context with growing complexity, the need for an integrative device for the highly differentiated unit multiplies. However, the only weekly forum for the professional staff of the HKCSS is usually adopted as a platform for report. Rarely is it used as a mechanism to discuss the organization's overall goals. While the monthly team meeting is better in serving the function of an interface device, the task of bringing a better interface between different teams heavily relies on the individual incident of co-operation, which can vary from time to time and person to person.

Growing Rigidity & Standardization

The alertness of different units in the need for exploring new roles and resources naturally brings them into more frequent and wider contact with the external environment. This poses stress and demands on the units of Development Team which has all along been performing supportive and technical functions such as the liaison with mass media by the Information Department to prepare press conferences and consultation given by the Research Department in the design and implementation of research initiated by Division's Committee.

This influx of demands from other units and the taking up of new roles itself inevitably lead to the need for prioritizing their work and establishing standard procedures so as to achieve better management of tasks. Formulation of procedures and work schedules are gradually taking place since 1991, starting from the first issue of Guidelines and Procedures of the Information Department. Similar practice is adopted in various departments of the Development Team and a conscious effort of updating or revising these documents follows.

Nevertheless, the growing rigidity runs contradictory to the adaptive measures of the other units, especially when timely response and immediate action to current issues are deemed necessary to bring the organization's effectiveness to public attention.

Blurring Boundary of Roles and Tasks

It may first seem to be self-contradictory for an organization to have both a high level of differentiation and a blurring boundary of roles and tasks simultaneously. However, this does happen in the HKCSS. While some of the roles are newly taken up or broken down, others roles which are originally played by a specific unit are taken up by another unit. This is largely a by-product of the growing rigidity mentioned above.

In view of the increasing lack of complementary functions of the two teams resulted from their own adaptive measures, some of the supportive functions originally taken by the Development Team are performed by the related Division of Agency Service Team. For example, getting contact with overseas organizations to plan for overseas study tours should originally be the task of the International and Regional Department while the translation of papers should originally be one of the tasks of the Information Department, and is now shared by other units in some incidents.

While it may be favourable for the units to co-operate and share tasks in case of emergency than sticking to the standardization of roles, the blurring of tasks in most of the times and the allowance for its continuity are in fact gradually redefining the roles of each other without formal recognition from the management nor consensus among colleagues. The scenario it creates only presents a further confusion in the existing turbulence.

Conclusion: The Way Ahead

It may be high time that the stress of contingency theory on the congruence between the structure and the environment be reiterated. The above analysis unfortunately presents a case where the adaptive measures taken are in fact detrimental as they leads to incongruence between the structure and the environment. While a structure with high differentiation complemented with adequate integrative device is called for, the development of differentiation is inconsistent and an integrative device dysfunctional; when a more flexible environment is necessary for different units to act timely, the opposite direction towards standardization and rigidity dominates.

The critical factor that brings about such incongruence and converting every goodwill into a destructive force may be the lack of awareness of the need and motivation for a concerted effort and development of a common organization goal geared towards the directions of the different units. Though it is still too lenient to excuse the various units by their pre-occupation with ever-increasing tasks, the blind-spot of the management level which is supposed to provide direction for the organization and lead the various units towards a unified target, has certainly played an important role in constructing the statuesque. What leads to the development of such a blind-spot? Should the inadequate integrative device be held accountable? Or is it an unexpected result of over-decentralization of decision-making authority?

It would be too rational and also too unrealistic to conclude that a total re-structuring of the existing organization will be the solution. Moreover, no matter how perfect that structure is designed in the management level, the implemented one will certainly present a discrepancy with the designed one. Therefore, it is only when the internal structure be perceived and analyzed just like the external environment can a breakthrough be possible. Same as its environment, merits of the existing structure can be perceived as resources for further consolidation, while the sources of causing the structure's instability should be identified and reduced. Only with a polished internal structure together with an updated understanding of the external environment can an organization proceed to formulate its goal, develop its adaptive strategy, and secure a consistent effort from all its staff.

References

Bargel, D. & Schmid, H. (ed) (1992) *Organizational Change and Development in Human Service Organizations*. Haworth Press.

Benson, J. Kenneth (1975) "The Interorganizational Network as a Political Economy". *Administrative Science Quarterly*, July 1975, Vol. 20, pp. 229–249.

Child, John (1977) *Organization: A Guide to Problems and Practice*. Harper & Row.

Hasenfeld, Yeheskel (ed) (1992) *Human Services as Complex Organization*. Sage Publication.

Hong Kong Council of Social Service Annual Report 1990–91.

Hong Kong Council of Social Service Annual Report 1991–92.

Hong Kong Council of Social Service Annual Report 1992–93.

Hong Kong Council of Social Service Annual Report 1993–94.

Hong Kong Government (March 1991) *Social Welfare into the 1990 and Beyond.*

Jhafritz, Jay M. and Ott, J. Steven (1992) *Classics of Organization Theory* (3rd Ed). Wadsworth.

Neugeboren, Bernard (1991) *Organization, Policy and Practice in the Human Service*. Haworth Press.

Pugh, D.S. & Hickson, D.J. (1989) *Writers on Organizations* (4th Ed). Penguin Books.

Scott, W. Richard (1992) *Organizations: Rational, Natural and Open Systems* (3rd Ed). Prentice-Hall, Inc.

5

Towards Total Quality in Community Rehabilitation Network: The Experience of Implementing Total Quality Management

Dominic CHUI, Kam Tong CHAN and Ivy HO

Introduction

Since the inauguration of the Community Rehabilitation Network (CRN) in April 1994, the importance of service quality has been emphasized. During the past eight years, the CRN has laid numerous ground-work on "quality" which aimed at cultivating the culture of quality in the CRN. The implementation of Total Quality Management (TQM) is regarded as the milestone on achieving Continuous Quality Improvement throughout the CRN, as it was stated unanimously in the the CRN Strategic Plan (1997–2000).

With the implementation of TQM, the CRN aimed at striving to be a quality driven organization which ensures the continuous improvement of service quality as well as fulfilling the needs and expectations of the service users. The commitment to high quality services in the CRN requires that all aspects of service to be managed and provided at the best possible level. They should meet the needs of the service users being served through efforts made continuously by all staff in the CRN. Service quality is in no way "new" to CRN, but the co-ordination and maximum recognition, reinforcement and increasing consistency of quality improvement via this venture perhaps are. In this paper, the quality journey of CRN will be described, starting from the formulation of the conceptual framework, strategies and time-frame for the implementation of TQM. The overview will then summarize the implementation of TQM during the past three years and some highlights on the future development will be made at the end of this paper.

Development of Community Rehabilitation Network

Community Rehabilitation Network is an innovative project administered by the Hong Kong Society for Rehabilitation with the mission to improve the quality of life of persons with chronic illness and their families. The CRN was established in response to the service gaps identified in the "Rehabilitation Green Paper" published in 1992. After years of piloting, the need for CRN was recognized in the "Rehabilitation White Paper" (1995) as an effective means to help persons with chronic illnesses and their family to re-integrate into society.

The project was officially launched in April 1994 and had been funded by the Jockey Club Charities for two years. During the pilot phase, two CRNs and a Clearinghouse had been established to provide services to persons with chronic illnesses and their families. Upon the completion of the pilot, the Lotteries Fund had been supporting the project until March 1997. Starting from1[st] April 1997, the Social Welfare Department has been providing regular funding to the three CRNs in Hong Kong Island, Kowloon East and Kowloon West. In the report of "Consultancy study on evaluation of CRN" published in 1999, the consultant has reaffirmed the importance and achievements of CRN and recommended that its service to be expanded to cover the whole territory.

Vision and Mission of Community Rehabilitation Network

In reviewing the experience of implementing the Total Quality Management (TQM) initiative, our first task was to revisit the vision and mission of the organization. A management workshop was organized with full participation of all frontline staff and senior management to discuss on the mission statement. In that workshop, we have examined both the general and the task environment affecting the patient services rendered by the CRN. We also have identified some of the critical issues that we needed to address. Thus, a revised vision and mission statement is as follows:

Our Vision

The Community Rehabilitation Network firmly believes that all persons with chronic illnesses and their families are entitled to abilities, rights and dignities. They possess a sense of competence in helping themselves and others to master their health, life and the environment. Based on the concepts of self-help and mutual support network, we are committed to provide high quality rehabilitation services and develop patient self-help groups in the community through innovative, flexible, caring and professional working approaches, which aim at optimizing their active participation in the rehabilitation process and policies formulation so as to enable them to resume to normal productive living and thus enhance their quality of life.

Our Mission

The **Mission** of the Community Rehabilitation Network is as follows:

Patients with chronic illnesses and families

- to meet and respond to the rehabilitative needs of individuals living in the community through the process of self-help, mutual help and empowerment

Patient self-help groups and organizations

- to provide dedicated support for their development, affirming the growth and consolidation of mutual-support networks to persons with chronic illnesses in the community

Staff

- to recognize our staff as our most valuable asset and enlist their total commitment on the provision of quality services through encouragement, involvement and training

Other agencies and bodies

- to optimize the use of resources in the community through interfacing and collaborating with related agencies and bodies

Public

- to advocate positive and caring attitudes towards persons with chronic illnesses in the community through sensitizing and educating the public to illness and disability issues

As mentioned in the revised mission statement, we want to provide an adequate coverage of all stakeholders, including the patients, self-help groups, staff and community partners. After the establishment of the mission statement, an action plan in implementing the TQM activities was developed accordingly.

Framework on Achieving Total Quality in Community Rehabilitation Network

Domains of Change Towards Achieving Total Quality

The TQM framework for any organization should be tailor-made and doctored to the specific characteristics and culture of that organization. Although the concepts of TQM are very simple and based on commonsense, developing and running a TQM project is actually a complex task. Before making the change to TQM, five domains of change, in the context of CRN, were identified and incorporated in the formulation of change strategies. The domains are:

Change in "Tasks"

This includes the incorporation of ideas and concepts of strategic planning and quality improvement planning, formulation of mission statement and quality strategy as well as conducting internal and external environmental scanning.

Change in "Structure"

This includes the modification and re-organization of existing administrative structure for the implementation of TQM such as the establishment of Quality Council, TQM Steering Committee, Quality Improvement Teams, Task Forces and TQM Co-ordinator.

Change in "People"

This includes the improvement of supervisory skills and competence of supervisors, development on effective teamwork and team building, conflict resolution ability, staff awareness, attitudes and empowerment on quality, effective communication culture, trust and integrity.

Change in "Technology"

This includes the acquisition of quality improvement techniques such as different quality tools and methods, effective communication skills, resources management and workload planning, skills in process re-engineering, service design, delivery and evaluation, customer servicing as well as development of performance indicators.

Change in "System"

This includes the establishment of quality systems on quality planning, quality control and standards setting, documentation, quality monitoring and review, co-ordination and evaluation of quality processes as well as the empowerment of quality systems.

Amalgamating the "changing domains" together with the five "quality strategies", the framework on implementing total quality in the CRN is formulated and shown in Fig. 1. It shows the three basic and important "building blocks" for TQM implementation, which were backed up by different quality improvement teams or taskforces and were directed by the mission vision as well as the strategic and quality plan of the CRN towards continuous quality improvement. Specifically, these three "blocks" of quality improvement activities are:

a. Customer-focused and oriented services: identify who the various customers/stakeholders of the service are and ensure high quality service is provided in response to feedback from various customers/ stakeholders.
b. Process re-engineering and improvement: ensures all processes both operational and support are clear, explicit and "controlled" in terms of standards, policies, procedures and protocols with regular monitoring and review.
c. Performance measurement, monitoring and evaluation: involves establishment of mechanisms in reviewing and monitoring the performance in service delivery.

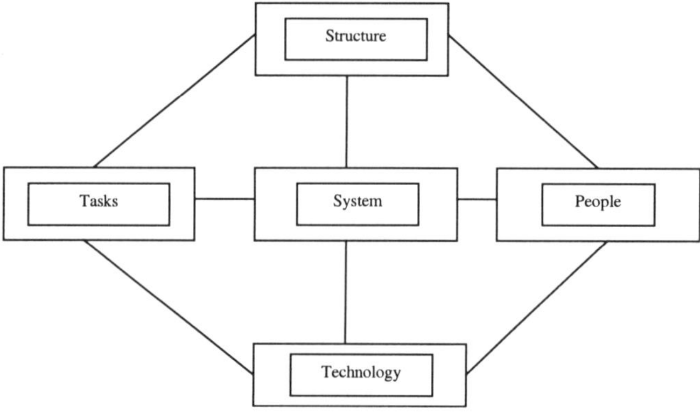

Fig. 1.

Strategies and Framework on Implementing Total Quality Management

With a clear purpose as to where the CRN is headed for total quality, the overall strategies (as shown in the Table 1) on implementing TQM are formulated so as to operationalize how total quality is to be accomplished in the CRN. The overall strategies on implementing TQM initiative include the following components:

a) Management Strategies
b) Communication Strategies
c) Training Strategies
d) Quality Improvement and Implementation Startegies
e) Quality Standard Setting, Monitoring and Review Strategies

Table 1: Strategy on the implementation of TQM in CRN.

Strategy	Objectives	Actions	Date of Implementation
1. Management Strategy To establish overall strategy and structure for development and implementation of TQM	To ensure the implementation of Total Quality Management by CRN	To formulate the CRN quality strategy for implementing TQM To form a TQM structure including the TQM Steering Committee, TQM Coordinator, Taskforces and Quality Improvement Teams as well as revamping the existing Quality Council To invite professionals as the CRN consultant in implementing TQM	Before October, 1997
2. Communication Strategy To develop comprehensive and effective communication system	To ensure that all staff and service users of CRN understand and communicate thoroughly on the development and effectiveness of implementing Total Quality Management	To develop regular communication channel throughout CRN outlining progress on TQM implementation and collect opinion from CRN staff To develop an explicit plan to communicate with the service users on progress of TQM implementation and establish effective mechanisms to understand their feedback and expectations on CRN service quality	From January, 1998
3. Training Strategy To formulate staff development and training policy for TQM	To provide appropriate training for CRN staff to ensure them to acquire knowledge and skills necessary in implementing Total Quality Management	To assess the training and development needs in implementing TQM and formulate a training and development plan/schedule for CRN staff To establish a TQM Resource Library to gather relevant information for reference To invite other professionals or institutes to provide related training	From July, 1997

Table 1. (*Continued*)

Strategy	Objectives	Actions	Date of Implementation
4. Quality Improvement and Implementation Strategy To develop mechanisms and plans for implementation of TQM	To formulate the details of implementing Total Quality Management so as to provide a clear direction for all CRN staff and units to improve service quality	To establish an evaluation mechanism in monitoring the effectiveness of implementing TQM To establish a documentation system for TQM To edit manual and guidelines for TQM To develop a staff appreciation scheme To encourage individual staff and unit to develop plan for improving service quality	From January, 1998
5. Quality Standard Setting; Monitoring and Review Strategy To establish monitoring and review mechanisms for TQM	To establish systems in monitoring and reviewing the standards and outcomes of CRN service	To develop a set of key CRN quality indicators with measurable standards and outcomes for each indicator To establish a monitoring and review mechanism to ensure maximum conformance to the CRN quality indicators	From July, 1999

Time Frame of the "Quality Journey"

The "Quality Journey" of the CRN was divided into three main phases, starting from 1997, with a different focus at each phase:

a. Formative phase (July 1997 to June 1998):
   In this initial phase, a number of elements which aimed at cultivating the quality consciousness as well as a changing culture were at work, such as the empowerment and training of staff on quality improvement, establishing and consolidation of quality structure, formulation of directions and strategies for quality improvement, training on effective teamwork and team building, improving customer service and feedback monitoring.

b. Action phase (July 1998 to June 1999):
   Following the momentum generated during the formative phase, different elements were then reinforced so that changes could be instilled into the organization. In order to encourage quality initiatives for all the professionals and supportive staff, new innovation and continuous quality projects were encouraged, such as quality oriented managerial and service breakthrough, service and process re-engineering, documentation and consolidation of standard practice procedures. A series of centred-based and individual re-engineering projects have been proposed and implemented. Up to now, there are totally three centre-based as well as 44 individual improvement projects being implemented.

c. Review and evaluation phase (July 1999 to June 2000):
   In this consolidation phase, elements with a focus on establishing systems in monitoring the standards and outcomes of service were included, such as the development of a checklist of quality indicators and standards, establishment of mechanisms for performance measurement and monitoring, and the use of peer review as well as quality audit. The main purpose of reviews and evaluation is to ensure a stablized quality assurance system for the on-going improvement activities.

Review of the "Quality Journey" from 1997 to 2000

With only the basic theoretical knowledge, limited manpower and funding resources as well as scarce experiences for reference in the area, the CRN still ventured on the quality journey five years ago. The major impetus was solely based on the commitment and accountability to different stakeholders including service users, funders, staff members, and other service providers as well as the general public.

In the formative phase, the most important milestone that the CRN had laid down was the modification of existing administrative structure to quality management structure such as the establishment of Quality Council, TQM Steering Committee, TQM Co-ordinator as well as various Quality Improvement Teams and Taskforces. The infrastructure was further reinforced with the formulation of a mission statement and a strategic plan as well as a quality strategy for the CRN which, in turn, provided an obvious future direction on continuous quality improvement and customer oriented services. Besides, through various events such as staff meetings, retreat workshops, staff training and development programs, the ideology of service quality and the quest for excellence were consistently injected into the CRN's quality culture.

The TQM is about the changing of organization culture and the way organizations used to be run, making them more responsive and customer focused. However, the success of improvement can only be linked to the incorporation and implementation of the process for continual improvement. Therefore, the establishment of quality improvement systems and the acquisition of various quality techniques were the major components in the action phase. The formation of four Quality Improvement Teams in different regional centers as well as two cross-center taskforces, the formulation of a total number of 44 Quality Improvement Projects from 1997 to 1999, the implementation of three focus groups to collect feedback and opinions of our service users, the establishment of a comprehensive CRN customer feedback system, and the conduction of a series of staff training workshops on process re-engineering, quality tools and methods, evidence-based practice, etc. all characterized the "hard-work" that the CRN had committed to in the action phase.

However, it was not a smooth journey while approaching the end of the action phase. In April 1999, with the implementation of Phase I Service Quality Standards (SQS) of the Service Performance Monitoring System (SPMS), the quality journey was temporarily detoured to focus on the development and implementation of a set "funder-laided and provider-led" quality standards. In a theoretical sense, the 19 SQSs consist of essential elements that constitute and are compatible with the CRN quality system. However, the "subvention implications" related to Phase I SQS implementation and assessment have resulted in the adjustment of the quality journey schedule of the CRN, especially the "Action" and "Review and evaluation phase".

The "Action phase" was extended to the second half of 1999 so as to accommodate the development, implementation and consolidation of the policy and procedures for the Phase I SQS. In line with this, elements on quality audit were more emphasized in the initial stage during the "Review and evaluation" phase so as to match with the timing of the SPMS's external assessment conducted by the Social Welfare Department. Moreover, the consolidation work on establishing systems in monitoring the standards and outcomes of service was only reactivated in the first quarter of 2000. Therefore, the CRN "Quality Journey" continued and extended until the "Review and evaluation phase" was completed in 2000.

Learning from past experiences, the CRN will review and refine the quality strategies from time to time so that the notion of "continuous quality improvement" can be accomplished effectively and realistically. Furthermore, in order to facilitate the achievement of a quality driven organization, the CRN will pay more effort in consolidating the quality culture that had been instilled among all colleagues, especially through the arrangement of staff sharing, appreciation and team-building occasions, participation in different quality improvement activities with emphasis on the "Small win approach", etc. The sense of "ownership" on improving service quality was initiated, developed and then consolidated.

In addition, with the implementation of Service Performance Monitoring System by the Social Welfare Department, the "adequacy" context of basic service quality is going to be addressed and guaranteed through the formulation of SQS related quality policy and procedures and the establishment of documentation system such as quality manual, standard operating procedures, etc. However, the "compliance" context should further be enforced, not only through the quality audit system operated by the Social Welfare Department, but also by the incorporation of organization-wide monitoring and review mechanism as well as the emphasis on "evidence-based practice" in the service delivery.

Through continuous reviews, monitoring and measurement of service quality, the CRN strives to be a quality driven organization which ensures the continuous improvement of the service quality as well as fulfilling the needs and expectations of service users.

References

Community Rehabilitation Network (1997) *Strategic Plan 1997–2000.* The Hong Kong Society for Rehabilitation.

Department of Community and Family Medicine (1999) *Consultancy Study on Evaluation of Community Rehabilitation Network.* The Chinese University of Hong Kong.

Green Paper on Rehabilitation (1992) *Equal Opportunities and Full Participation: A Better Tomorrow for All.* Hong Kong, Government Printer.

White Paper on Rehabilitation (1995) *Equal Opportunities and Full Participation: A Better Tomorrow for All.* Hong Kong, Government Printer.

6

Continuous Quality Improvement (CQI) in Grantham Hospital

Dr. S. C. LEUNG, Hospital Chief Executive, Grantham Hospital
Ms. M. L. CHAN, CQI Coordinator, Grantham Hospital

The journey to better quality has been undertaken by the Grantham Hospital, a 600-bed cardiothoracic centre, since 1993. Parallel to the introduction of new management structure to improve accountability, the Continuous Quality Improvement (CQI) concept was gradually introduced. Through a prolonged educational process of a cascading programme, senior managers, middle managers and front-line staff are totally involved. The establishment of a quality management structure is unique and is integrated into the overall management structure. Through empowerment by education, staff become leaders in their teams and take initiatives. Many creative ideas come true and processes are reengineered, resulting in better coordination between departments and therefore better patient care.

Patients ready for discharge find that they have to wait for over five hours before they can obtain the drugs to take home. Operation Theatre staff waste time on waiting for the first patient to arrive and other preparatory work before they can start a day's work. Since their daily procedures in the hospital are established in "old ways", it would be difficult for health carers to deliver a level of health care that they wish to attain.

For Grantham Hospital, a centre receiving referrals from hospitals for treatment of complex heart and lung diseases for adults and children, a management philosophy to streamline procedures, maximise efficiency and reduce work would facilitate the delivery of a consistent level of quality patient care.

To achieve the objective of providing quality patient care and quality hospital services, the Grantham Hospital is integrated in the public hospital service of the Hospital Authority in 1991. The introduction of new management structure was started in November 1992 with the appointment of a Hospital Chief Executive (HCE). The objective of this structure is to provide a proper framework with clear lines of management accountability in order to improve the efficiency of hospital service for the benefit of patients. The basic functional unit for delivery of clinical service is the ward. The core of the organisation structure of the clinical service division is an integrated clinical team (ICT). The team consists of medical staff in the clinical department and nursing and supporting staff in the associated wards. There are three levels of managers in the team — the Chief of Service (COS), the Department Operations Manager (DOM) or Department Manager (DM) and the Ward Manager (WM) in those departments. The hospital has three other divisions: Nursing, Administration, and Finance, and all are headed by General Managers (GM). The HCE will have overall responsibility for the management of the hospital, with the GMs and COS being accountable to the HCE.

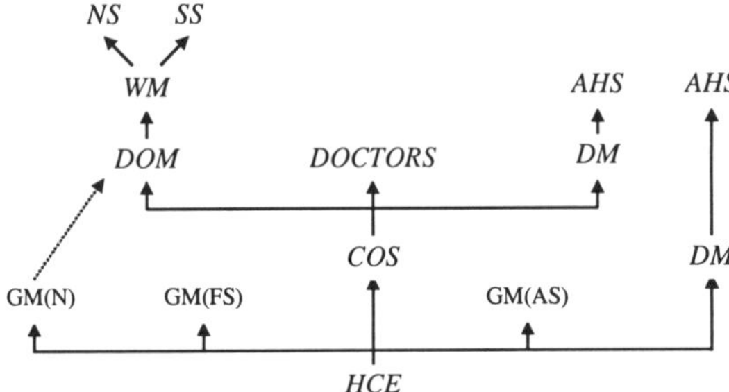

HCE = Hospital Chief Executive	DOM = Department Operations Manager
GM(N) = General Manager (Nursing)	WM = Ward Manager
GM(FS) = General Manager (Finance Services)	AHS = Allied Health Staff
GM(AS) = General Manager (Administration Services)	NS = Nursing Staff
COS = Chief of Service	SS = Supporting Staff
DM = Department Manager	

Fig. 1. Hospital management structure.

Underpinning the new management structure is the new management culture and philosophy which emphasizes the following:

a) focus on the front-line operating units;
b) multidisciplinary team approach to patient care;
c) clear line of management accountability;
d) participatory management culture; and
e) greater public participation in the provision of hospital services.

By focusing on the front-line operating units in the hospital where most of the activities take place, the new culture emphasizes a patient-focused approach in the delivery of hospital services. Doctors, nurses, allied health professionals and other supporting staff would work together to achieve common goals. In working together as a multiidisciplinary team, there is a need for open and honest communication. Set on this background, there is a definite advantage to integrate the CQI approach which is based on the improvement of processes and systems. Total involvement, customer-focus and continuous improvement are important philosophies propelling the new management initiatives.

There must be a headstart for all these efforts. Particularly in the face of the new management structure being introduced, the integration of the CQI into day-to-day work poses a challenge.

Phase I: Preparatory Stage 1992–1993

Instilling the concept of the CQI into the staff is a continuous process and it is of paramount importance to start with the senior managers. It is crucial for the HCE to assume a leading and mentoring role in coaching and encouraging the senior managers. The first year was mainly a preparation period for the CQI to be fully implemented in the Grantham Hospital. The year's activities focused on communication, integration and coordination.

Communication

A survey was conducted in early 1993 in which 93 senior managers ranked "Quality Patient-centred Care" as the core value. Throughout

1993, the concept of quality as well as the CQI was infused into all staff and the Hospital Governing Committee through activities such as briefings, slogan competition and seminar.

Integration

The CQI concept should be integrated into the infrastructure of the hospital. A mission statement developed by senior managers reflected the aspiration of the Grantham Hospital in providing quality patient-centred care. Regular patient satisfaction survey was introduced to obtain regular customer feedback. With the introduction of the new management structure in November 1993 upon the appointment of the GM, COS, DOM, and the DM, guidance and support were given by the HCE in the form of interpersonal briefing on the CQI and the groundwork to be laid down to form a basis for the CQI work in the department committee/integrated clinical team. Such tools include establishing clinical and non-clinical quality indicators and trending of such data and trend tables to detect variations. A hospital-wide incident report system was introduced to track and act on any preventable or unexpected events with effects which could have affected the safety of patients, safety of staff, patient's rights, hospital's public relations, complaints, management process, work policies, equipment design, communications, etc.

As the new management structure was being established, the CQI concept was put in place early in the work of functional departments; trending of department workloads and performance indicators, patient care indicators, etc were established so that a data base is set up to monitor performance in achieving business plans and identify areas for improvement. Hospital cumulative outcome data collection to be monitored in ICT and at the Hospital Management Committee and Hospital Governing Committee level helps health carers to note the best performance based on the data, to learn from that performance and to improve with the goal of meeting or exceeding this level.

Coordination

With many of the committee structure in place eg. Hospital Management and Medical Committee, these became good forums to reinforce the concept of the CQI. In a survey conducted in August 1993, opportunity was taken to measure the clinical management teams' view on their effectiveness in enabling the concepts of quality better understood, facilitation of patient-centred care and efficiency and effectiveness in fulfilling the need of patients. The result was encouraging; the majority of ICTs self-rated high scores to these variables.

A hospital improvement subcommittee was formed in December 1992 to suggest key improvement areas and monitor improvement achievements. It was chaired by the HCE and members including senior management as well as front-line doctors, nurses and allied health staff. General improvements and special projects were initiated. The former were *ad hoc* and short-term improvements in eg. ward environment, customer service, signage, visiting hours, patient satisfaction survey, communication with staff, etc. The basic concepts of the CQI were also discussed. For the ICTs which were put into trial in April 1993 and fully implemented in November 1993, there were also many improvements in work process and communication. A cross-functional improvement project brought marked improvements in the Specialist Out-patient Department service.

Phase II: Behaviour Modification Stage January to June 1994

Since one of the focuses of the CQI is process reengineering, another effort to bring about improvement on work process was launched by early 1994. Three workshops on "Restructuring Hospital Operations to Improve Quality of Care and Performance" were conducted by the HCE to 102 middle and front-line nursing and allied health staff. The aim was to understand the need for change, identify issues and suggest solutions. In these workshops, not only was a two-way communication between managers and staff established, many ideas and issues requiring reengineering of processes — nursing procedures, supply, checking, centralization of catering, meal delivery, portering services etc. — were generated by the workshop participants. Many of the concepts on training, communication, elimination of unnecessary or non-value added works and staff welfare were shared. The HCE and senior management took on these suggestions and facilitated, supported or planned and implemented many improvements suggested during the workshops. Details are as follows:

- Introduction of Health Care Assistant
- Enhancement and coordination of nursing training
- Introduction of core induction training for doctors and nurses
- Introduction of continuous night allowance
- Introduction of denursing programmes
- Introduction of disposable sputum mug
- Reduction on unnecessary linen items
- Review of accountable drug list and minimisation of drug check
- Extension of pharmacy service during long weekends or public holidays
- Review of pre- and post-operation routines
- Reduction on overbooking of OT and Catheterization Laboratory List
- Standardisation of doctor preference at OT
- Installation of fax machines for X-ray orders
- Introduction of phone order for emergency X-ray
- Centralisation of meals delivery
- Centralisation of cleansing
- Centralisation of patient delivery
- Rescheduling of CSSD collection time-table
- Improvement in organisation of life service
- Improvement on security of rear entrance
- Introduction of thermometer sheath
- Standardisation of syringe pump
- Review of frequency of changing IV drip set, respiratory tubing and peritoneal dialysis sets
- Improvement in preparation for new roles among NO/RN/WM after introduction of new management structure
- Enhanced improvement in nursing quarters environment
- Installation of air-conditioning in call rooms
- Improvement in transportation during typhoon
- Introduction of cleaning programme for air-conditioners
- Improvement in QA — performance indicators, patient outcomes, accident reports, patient education
- Review of nursing procedures eg. pre-operation bath frequency
- Involvement of relatives in pediatric patient care
- Installation of better positioned sockets in pediatric patient care

- Introduction of appropriate checking and decentralization of inventory items
- Review of CSSD preset instrument packs
- Introduction of new procedure on exchange and requisition of reusable CSSD articles
- Review of procedures for returned drugs — to be processed by pharmacist
- Review of preparation check nursing procedure
- Revision of ID ring checking procedure
- Revision of wound checking nursing procedure
- Review of mask changing procedure
- Simplification of last office procedure
- Simplification of temperature chart
- Improvement in statistical definition of in-patient
- Revision of bed sheet and pillow cases change frequency
- Cancellation of full lead ECG for dead patients
- Review of in and out charting procedure, elimination of water measure for in and out charts
- Revision of towel preparation
- Revision of consent signing procedure
- Introduction of bilingual OT and Catheterization Laboratory list
- Improvement in filling system
- Enhancing in-service training by doctors
- Introduction of 24-hour hot water supply
- Centralization of supplies/procurement
- Establishment of monthly meeting for DOM/WM/NO/EN
- Introduction of streamline sick leave certificate issue procedure
- Setting up of recreation/garden for patients
- Introduction of customer service training for front-line staff
- Minimisation of waiting time for repairs
- Establishment of staff Club
- Revision of signage
- Review of public telephone service — introduction of semi-private bed
- Improvement in image of X-ray and Clinical Physiology Laboratory

This phase is characterised by actual actions or behaviours to restructure or reengineer procedures or operations to improve the quality of service. To be more effective, it is necessary for the management to be able to ask the front-line staff how to make things better. There was, however, a lack of formal exposure to CQI or technical tools to implement the CQI.

Phase III: Reinforcement and Consolidation Stage Since July 1994

By mid-1994, although the success of the workshops seemed to have brought the hospital forward, there was concern as to the actual diffusion of the CQI concept to all our staff. There were insights that a lot of CQI activities were going on but were not focused and systematic enough. There was a lack of direction and structure for implementation. A hospital mission statement had been introduced in 1992 and revised in 1993 but CQI activities were not explicitly linked to it. The vision statement was not adequately communicated to staff. It was not audience-friendly. There was a lack of hospital-based training and guidance from professionals. The success may not be perpetuated without an internalization of or reinforcement on CQI. Commitment of senior managers alone was not enough; there was a need for knowledge and skill, and a wider coverage for middle and front-line staff. In July 1994, the need to provide a knowledge-based support and skills training on CQI tools was evident and a local consultancy was appointed to facilitate reinforcement and provide guidance. The hospital mission and direction was clarified by the collective wisdom of the senior team. An in-hospital training session was conducted for senior managers. The professional input on concepts and perspectives on total quality and the five basic elements of CQI including leadership, customer focus, continuous improvement, total involvement and process reengineering enhanced the motivation and commitment of the senior team. The senior managers, having familiarized themselves with quality improvement before formally launching the initiative to cascade to the middle managers who in turn, reach out to the front-line staff. Involving the COS as physician leaders at this stage can help to build up a "critical mass" of support among physicians. In parallel, a structure to support CQI activities was established.

This included establishment of the CQI Steering Committee, CQI Leadership Council, CQI Project Team and continuous improvement teams (CIT). Chartered formats to document CQI and CIT projects were put into use. A CQI resource centre was established. The CQI structure was integrated into the existing management structure and also allowed cross-functional involvement. In this way, the CQI effort was integrated with the hospital mission and there was better use of team work and participative management to move the hospital forward. Tools for diffusion of the CQI concept was developed to cascade from senior managers to middle management and front-line staff. Major roadblocks, eg. professional staff, resources and team work were identified. Senior teams are committed to integrate efforts to overcome them.

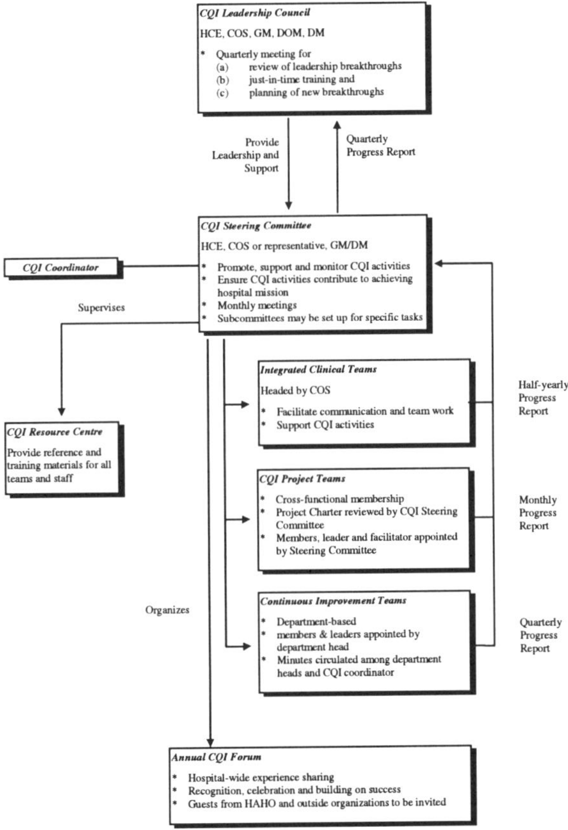

Fig. 2. CQI structure.

This phase was characterised by the taking on of CQI as a management responsibility by the managers. There are a focus and a system to ensure continuous improvement. Initiation by ICTs and successful implementation of CQI or CIT projects flourished.

Process	Indicator	Improvement	Benefit
• Provision of drugs from Pharmacy to wards	• Cycle time	• Reduction in cycle time	• Reduction of waste of nursing staff time • Better care for patients • Reduction in discharge time: Patient and staff satisfaction; Better utilization of Pharmacy staff
• Clinical protocol revision	• Groin complication • Utilization of cross-matched blood • Fresh frozen plasma • Incidence of sub-acute bacterial endoceditis	• Stent protocol: Decrease in groin complication • Catheter protocol: Decrease in cross-matched blood • Warfarin overdose: Decrease in fresh frozen plasma usage • Dental protocol: Decrease in sub-acute	• Better patient care • Better doctor-nurse communication • unnecessary errors avoided • Better guidance for junior doctors
• Pre-operation preparations	• Delay in starting the first operation	• Punctual starting of the first operation • the preparation time shortened by 30%	• Better services for patients • Better utilization of nursing manpower (1096 hours) • Saving of 237 doctor hours wasted on waiting • Better utilization of OT sessions • Job enrichment for OTA and clerical staff

Fig. 3. (*continued*)

Process	Indicator	Improvement	Benefit
• Issuance of sterile articles from CSSD	• Wastage of nursing manpower	• Reduction of ward nursing time spending on this procedure by 80% to 90% • Reduction of cycle time (in CSSD) for checking of the used CSSD articles by 80%	• Saving of nursing manpower • Improvement of CSSD services • Improvement of hospital environment at corridors in front of OT and CSSD • Better utilization of the hospital elevators
• Provision of central delivery of patient meals	• Cycle time	• Reduction of cycle time by 70% and saving of manpower by 75% (Ward Attendant man-hour per day)	• Alleviation of workload of Ward Attendant to assist in performing nursing duties • Better utilization of lift services • Reduction of waste of nursing staff time
• Provision of centralized procurement services to wards and departments/units	• Cycle time • percentage of assets managed	• Reduction of nursing/allied health manpower involving in procurement matters by 20%	• Reduction of nursing/allied health staff in procurement matters • Better control and monitoring on procurement matters
• Installation of a new PABX telephone system with linkage to internal paging system	• Cycle time required for response to paging • Requirement of Telephone Operator	• Reduction of cycle time by 25% and saving of manpower (ie Telephone Operator) by 50% (from 4 to 2)	• Improvement in communications
• Establishment of a central inventory records register for the whole hospital	• Percentage of assets managed	• Better care of physical assets • Order of supplies are well controlled	• Better utilization of resources • Better monitoring of inventories • Better planning of future replacement/ procurement programme

Fig. 3. Examples from process quality improvement

During the period from July to October 1994, a total number of 74 CIT projects have either been planned or implemented, including 25 projects which have been completed in October 1994. The improvement activities are varied and addressed the improvement needs of various units/departments.

Unit	Improvement activities	Progress (as on 31.10.94)
1 CCU	Patients' bed bathing time	Completed
2 CCU	Expanded role of BTTA nurses in CCU	Data collection stage
3 CCU	Patients satisfaction survey in CCU	Planning stage
4 Chest Surgical	Pain control of post-operation patients	Data collection stage
5 Chest Surgical	Staff satisfaction survey	Planning stage
6 Orthopaedic	Taking patients' temperature	Evaluation stage
7 Orthopaedic	Patient assisted bathing time	Evaluation stage
8 Orthopaedic	Prevention of dislocation on post hip replacement patients	Implementation stage
9 Orthopaedic	Reorganisation of ward routine after renovation	Data collection stage
10 Cardiac & General Medical	Booking of NEATS/ambulance	Completed
11 Cardiac & General Medical	Filling in obs charts, urine tests, body weight	Completed
12 Cardiac & General Medical	Sending of ECG and x-ray request forms	Completed
13 Cardiac & General Medical	Sending of laboratory specimens	Implementation stage
14 Cardiac & General Medical	MSW waiving request procedures	Data collection stage
15 Cardiac & General Medical	Cardiac catheterization - sending of patients	Data collection stage
16 Cardiac & General Medical	Internal transfer: case reporting	Data collection stage
17 Specialist Out-patient	Stock drug review	Data collection stage
18 Cardiac Paediatric	Patient/parent satisfaction survey	Evaluation stage
19 Cardiac Paediatric	Medical record filing system	Data collection stage
20 Cardiac Paediatric	Admission process	Data collection stage
21 Main Kitchen	Setting up of standard recipes for soup	Implementation stage
22 X-Ray	Renovation of a washroom to patients' changing room	Completed
23 X-Ray	Upgrading of old changing cubicle	Completed
24 X-Ray	Two 3-seater sofas, wooden bench and pictures added	Completed

Fig. 4. (*continued*)

Unit		Improvement activities	Progress (as on 31.10.94)
25	X-Ray	Improvement in communication with patients by installation of intercom	Completed
26	X-Ray	Installation of TV and sound system	Planning stage
27	X-Ray	CQI workshop for supervisors	Completed
28	X-Ray	Magazine rack in staff room	Completed
29	X-Ray	Quality control of x-ray images	Planning stage
30	Clinical Physiology	Attendance for CQI workshop of all allied health staff	Completed
31	Clinical Physiology	departmental mission statement finalized	Completed
32	Clinical Physiology	Cosy atmosphere in Respiratory Laboratory created	Evaluation stage
33	Physiotherapy (Ortho)	Education pamphlet for patients after THR	Completed
34	Physiotherapy (Ortho)	Monitoring of pressure sore and identification of risk	Data collection stage
35	Physiotherapy (Ortho)	Revision of nursing care on patients after THR	Completed
36	Physiotherapy (Ortho)	Construction of a new form to monitor the progress of patients after TKR	Completed
37	Physiotherapy (Ortho)	Production of education board in the corridor of Orthopaedic Ward	Planning stage
38	Pathology	CQI concept, cascading	Implementation stage
39	Pathology	Improvement in laboratory courier service	Planning stage
40	Pathology	Improvement in turnaround time of liver and renal profile tests	Completed
41	Administration Services	Centralization of portering services	Planning stage
42	Central Nursing Division	Process reengineering — nursing staff and pupil nurse allocation	Planning stage
43	Central Nursing Division	Streamlining of borrowing procedure and extension of library opening hours	Planning stage
44	Physiotherapy	Establishment of procedure manual in Pulmonary Rehabilitation Programme (PRP) (Physiotherapy guidelines)	Implementation stage
45	Physiotherapy	Protocol guideline for pre and post operation physiotherapy routine for surgical patients	Completed
46	Physiotherapy	Evaluation of follow-up intervals for PRP Out-patients Department patients	Data collection stage
47	Physiotherapy	Evaluation of effects of ex-tolerance for PRP patients	Data collection stage
48	Physiotherapy	Home exercise programme for PRP patients after discharge	Implementation stage

Fig. 4. (*continued*)

Unit		Improvement activities	Progress (as on 31.10.94)
49	Physiotherapy	Evaluation of ADL assessment form in PRP unit	Implementation stage
50	Physiotherapy	Questionnaire on satisfaction and expectation of in-patients in PRP unit	Data collection stage
51	Physiotherapy	Construction of a quiz for patients in PRP	Implementation stage
52	Physiotherapy	Revision of procedure on treadmill training programme	Completed
53	Physiotherapy (Cardiac)	Data-base formation for future improvement	Data collection stage
54	Physiotherapy (Cardiac)	Regular academic presentation by members	Implementation stage
55	Physiotherapy (Cardiac)	Formulation of unit mission statement	Completed
56	Physiotherapy (Cardiac)	Guidelines for Sunday and public holiday working list	Completed
57	Physiotherapy (Cardiac)	Supervision guidelines	Implementation stage
58	Physiotherapy (Cardiac)	Participating in COC, ICU and rehabilitation QA group to promote the implementation of CQI	Implementation stage
59	Physiotherapy (Paediatric sub-group)	Service development to include gross motor departmental programmes	Implementation stage
60	Physiotherapy (Paediatric sub-group)	Service guidelines on assessment in NICU	Completed
61	Physiotherapy (Paediatric sub-group)	Service guidelines on pre-operation programmes	Completed
62	Physiotherapy (Paediatric sub-group)	Delivery of a talk on Cardiac & Chest Physiotherapy in Guangzhou	Planning stage
63	Physiotherapy (Paediatric sub-group)	Competence based on job coaching	Implementation stage
64	Physiotherapy (Paediatric sub-group)	Linkage with other physiotherapy out-patient centres for referral purposes	Implementation stage
65	Physiotherapy (Paediatric sub-group)	Participation in multidisciplinary ward round	Implementation stage
66	Physiotherapy (Paediatric sub-group)	Setting up of a cardiac rehabilitation protocol in phase II	Implementation stage
67	Physiotherapy (Paediatric sub-group)	Provision of exercise guidelines for patients before discharge	Completed
68	Physiotherapy (Paediatric sub-group)	Pre-operation phamplet for cardiac surgical patients	Completed
69	Tuberculosis & Chest	TB patients' satisfaction feedback questionnaire	Implementation stage

Fig. 4. (*continued*)

Unit		Improvement activities	Progress (as on 31.10.94)
70	Tuberculosis & Chest	Quality of life assessment from small cell lung carcinoma patients	Implementation stage
71	Tuberculosis & Chest	Asthma patients' feedback questionnaire	Implementation stage
72	Tuberculosis & Chest	Information sheets for patients on percutaneous needle lung biopsy, fibreoptic bronchoscopy, lymph node biopsy	Completed
73	Tuberculosis & Chest	Information sheets for patients on pleural tapping, insertion of pleural drain bone marrow biopsy and abdominocenteses	Planning stage
74	Tuberculosis & Chest	Structured junior doctors's mentorship programme	Implementation stage

Fig. 4. Summary on CIT quarterly (July–October 1994) progress report

During a reunion workshop with senior managers, the lessons and benefits of the programme in cascading the CQI concept from senior managers to middle managers and then front-line staff were discussed. An unanimous view is that the programme has enhanced communication and team spirit among different departments. There has been total involvement in the process and the movement has resulted in shared mission and value among staff. There has been empowerment of authority and this increased the job satisfaction of our staff, who are being assured that creative ideas can come true. A common language has been developed and a clear direction has been established. The importance of listening to the unheard is realized. It has also been agreed in the workshop that the CQI movement should be an on-going process and it is time-consuming to overcome resistance to changes. On-going evaluation is also necessary for continuous improvement.

"Pockets" of Staff Population Requiring Special Attention

There has always been a concern on how to bring the message of the CQI to all the front-line workers. Cascading workshops need to be modified both in language and simplicity particularly for those front-line staff of supporting service. The plan is to integrate the CQI concept into the Customer Service training programme for them.

Early involvement of COS and clinician ensure continuous improvement of health outcome. Strong and visible commitment by the COS, as senior manager of the ICT, should show that quality improvement is a serious effort and a top organisational priority. Membership of COS in both the Steering Committee and the Quality Council and their leading role in the ICT appointing and monitoring CIT will ensure that physician concerns are addressed in quality improvement. Clinical manifestation of their interest in improving quality of care are clinical care protocols and guidelines (Fig. 3). Clinician involvement in team effort to improve infectious disease control and blood transfusion procedure are just some concrete examples of their active participation.

Conclusion

In leadership for CQI breakthrough, the major challenge is total involvement in process reengineering to bring about continuous improvement through customer-focused approach. Only through enhanced leadership and commitment by the HCE and the support of knowledge and skills, senior and middle management can create ownership of CQI challenge and bring about attitude change among all staff through education and peer learning could the ultimate goal of achieving best care for patient through best practice be achieved.

References

Joint Commission on Accreditation of Healthcare Organizations (1993) *Implementing Quality Improvement: A Hospital Leader's Guide*.
Management Division, Hospital Authority (April 1992) *Manual on Hospital Management Structure*.

7

The Implementation of Case Management Model: A Way Ahead for a Better Service Delivery System in Medical Social Service

TSOI Yuen Kan

Introduction

A hospital is a multi-disciplinary setting aimed at providing "total patient care" through the cooperation among different professions which perform their respective functions and roles. Its emphasis is on ensuring clients' quality of life and their possibility to benefit from "community care". Medical social workers, forming one of the allied health professions, are responsible for dealing with the psycho-social needs and problems of patients and their families.

With the transfer of control from the Health Department to the Hospital Authority (HA), hospital service has become more comprehensive. The Medical Social Work Department (MSWD) has expanded accordingly to meet the increasing demands, and so have other allied health professions. Given this opportunity for expansion, both in manpower and structure, the MSWD has also undergone the pressure from other allied health professions to redefine its services boundaries — a base for them to fight for internal resources.

Social Workers, as professionals in providing counseling service, have to describe their tasks more precisely as the first step towards providing good quality services. Thus administrative problems are identified and a mini action research is carried out to examine the possibility of improving the current services delivery system through employing the framework and useful tools of case management model suggested by Ballew & Mink (1986).

Current Situation

With the supportive attitude and recognition of our importance from the Hospital Chief Executive, the MSWD benefits from the expansion of hospital service, both in terms of its staff and structure. Its number of staff increases from eight in 1988 to 13 in 1992 and is projected for 16 in 1994. Its structure also changes to a more complex one: from one SWO to seven ASWOs in 1988 to two SWOs to 11 ASWOs in 1992. A "casework supervisor" is added in-between the officer-in-charge and front-line staff. The officer-in-charge is formally appointed as Department Manager in early 1994. The hierarchy as well as the supervisory and administrative roles become more well defined.

The increase in manpower is obviously contributory. It confirms the importance of medical social service in hospital administration and offers an opportunity to develop, apart from the traditional casework approach, another stance in handling clients' needs/problems.

However, there are weaknesses in the MSWD that need to be addressed. Structural changes do not solve the problem of difference in case handling practice among front-line staff. Great variations, either in ways of case handling or criteria of providing clients with community resources, invite a lot of comparisons and complaints from clients. The quality of service is perceived as unstable and heterogeneous, if not substandard.

To address this problem, the guideline/manual governing the service delivery is looked for. It turns out to be an unattended messy file in the cabinet. The information inside is out-dated. It takes no notice of the recent changes such as medical consultation fee, criteria for referral and procedure for getting community resources. Besides, its content is far from comprehensive. The procedure and steps described are very brief and no criterion for professional consideration was provided.

As no adequate written guideline is available, the staff always have to turn to the casework supervisor for advice on action to be taken. Her personal and professional quality as well as the willingness of the staff to discuss the case with her, definitely affect the standardization of service quality. With the increase of supervisor to staff ratio (i.e. 1:14 in mid 1994), it may exceed her capacity to accommodate all the individual differences. Although it may be argued that such practice allows high flexibility and autonomy, the quality of service relies heavily on the morale of staff, their experience, knowledge and skills, and the casework supervisor's control.

Faced with the above administrative loophole, the front-line staff has actually cried for a standardization of service, i.e., to consolidate the service domain and to highlight the functions and tasks of Medical Social Workers, especially when new staff is going to be recruited. It is extremely difficult for a new staff to realize what service quality is expected from him/her. Much time has to be spent on orientating him/her and in his/her own familiarization with the availability of community resources. Such a period of trial and error gives him/her much frustration and anxiety. The cost is great and the effectiveness of the service delivery is undermined.

On the other hand, the MSWD has to spend more and more time on the clarification and discussion of criteria and procedure in case handling. Such time can definitely be saved through setting up of an operational manual for the staff's reference. Unfortunately, the Department is unable to make use of its opportunity to achieve a better service. Further to our dismay, it fails to meet unjustifiable external challenges from other multi-disciplinary team members. For instance, physiotherapists try to define some of the social work tasks like stress management into their daily practice, despite their weak professional justification. This is by no means a negligible threat to the MSWD. It is time for the administrator to think over the strategy on how to respond.

Rationale for the Action Research

With the above scenario, we may try to verify if the service delivery system of the MSWD can be improved and presented precisely through employing the concept, the comprehensive framework of analysis and the useful tools (eco-map, service agreement, resources file) of case management model.

The Case Management Model

Its Characteristics

As a model for human services, the ultimate goal of case management is to connect the client with needed helpers (Ballew & Mink, 1986, p. 15) and to enable him to get and use help effectively. The presence of their need for help is due to the presence of multiple problems which leads to their unsatisfying or unproductive life. To analyze the client's situation, it looks into the person-environment transactions through a system perspective. Its purpose is to look for the possible resource arrangement to fulfill a client's needs or resolve his problems.

Case management places its primary focus on the service/resource network. It concentrates on developing/enhancing a resource network; and strengthening clients personal competence to obtain and use the resources (Ballew & Mink, 1986, p. 3). Medical social service, with similar emphasis, also relies heavily on the community resources to achieve the treatment goals with the clients and look for strengthening the quality of their community life. Resource networking actually had to be done in two directions. The first is to coordinate social services from multiple agencies (formal networking) and the second is to mobilize help from their families, friends and volunteers (informal networking). Equal attention has to be paid to them.

Practically, the case management model can be viewed as a service delivery model. It helps to describe "a plan or a pattern which can serve as a framwork for the work you do for your clients" (Ballew & Mink, 1986, p. 9). It is also a set of procedure to assist social workers to work with the clients. It can be used as a tool and its application will be determined by the creativity of the user. Furthermore, it allows flexible employment as a guide that it has to complement with social work process and professional judgment, and it is up to individual staff members to adjust and fit the characteristics of each client.

The case management model is found to be very complementary to medical social service in hospital. Medical social workers, though equipped with professional knowledge and skills, have to rely heavily on external resources to handle the crisis of individuals and their families. Their crisis usually implies multiple problems and their inability to cope with them. The case management model can be fitted into the social work process and enable the clients to face and cope with their problems effectively through working out a comprehensive plan on the necessary social services and enlist the assistance from several helpers at once. Medical social workers pay a significant role to liaise with community resources and pay effort in coordinating the fragmented social services, maximizing existing resources and promoting the development of new resources.

The case management model works out six stages (Appendix I) to tackle clients' problems. Engagement is the first stage which is a process of building a helping relationship with the client. Assessment is the second stage which tries to identify the needs and demands, resources and capabilities in the clients' life. Planning, the third stage, emphasizes the process to set goals with clients and plan for action. The fourth stage is to formulate strategies for accessing resources and to involve the clients in developing a resource utilization plan so as to achieve the goals effectively and efficiently. Coordinating is the fifth stage which aims at adjusting the flow of resources and enabling the task implementation. After the above stages have been carried out and the results are evaluated, it enters into the disengagement stage and the helping process will be terminated.

Yet, the above process is not a linear process. It is a circular flow (Appendix II) as clients' problems may appear again when they face another crisis of changes in social condition. Applied into the medical setting, Appendix III shows the core tasks done in its circular flow. Yet, the spiral effect of the case management process does not need to be neglected as the achievement of a service plan does not imply a solution to prevent all the problems from arising in future.

In addition to the conceptual framework, the case management model is implemented through some useful tools which can be applied in daily practice.

a) An eco-map (Appendix IV) helps to analyze the client's transaction with his task environment and reflects the problem area easily for intervention.

b) A service agreement, in either verbal or written form, is a contract of mutual understanding on the goals and actions.

c) A resources file is organized to store the up-dated information for workers' quick reference.

Mini-survey on Current Practice — The Prerequisite of Case Management Design

A mini action research is conducted among the front-line staff. In addition to the personal contacts to gather their perceived advantages and disadvantages of the present practice they are invited to fill in a questionnaire. The objective is to ask for their feedback on clients' needs and problems commonly tackled and to have their task analyzed from daily practice and the resources commonly connected. Besides, their opinions and recommendation for future improvement are collected. Furthermore, the statistics of caseload and nature of problems from January to December 1993 would be studied. With reference to this information, an operational manual will be drafted as a reminder according to the concept of case management model.

The front-line staff is very supportive to participate in the mini-research. It can be reflected from the 100% return rate of the questionnaire.

The first part is to look for the commonality of the elderly clients in the hospital. It is found that five out of nine workers handle over 61% elderly cases. Three out of these five deal with 81% to 100% elderly cases. This reflects that the elderly clients are one of the largest consumers of health care services and represent a significant proportion of the MSWD's total caseload. To choose the elderly clients as the target for the first operational manual is therefore justifiable. Once their needs and problems are handled in an effective and efficient way, it implies a good quality of service.

The second part is to ask the staff to list the needs and concerns of the elderly cases according to their importance. Home care arrangement is found to be the most needy task. Financial hardship is weighted as the second most important issue to be handled. The third pressing problem is the need to arrange for institutional care and accommodation as well as management of their emotional response to illness. Management of resources, personality and relationship problems are regarded as the fourth important area. The fifth significant concern is to identify the unknown cases and enhance the clients' communication with the medical team.

Among the various needs and problems, the core tasks performed are analyzed according to the time spent. Needs and problems assessment is regarded as the most common task to be achieved daily. To set service goal(s) with clients and to develop an action plan are the second most important work. The third and fourth important tasks are to look for the appropriate resources, make referrals and arrange discharge plans. Relatively, MSWs spend the least time in evaluating results and terminating cases.

As medical social workers control no community resources, it is necessary for them to connect clients with the community resources so as to achieve the service goals. Thus, they are asked to list the most frequently employed resources in order of time spent. The answers in descending order are (1) financial help; (2) home care services; (3) institutional care; (4) rehousing/accommodation and counseling service; (5) employment service and educational/developmental programs; (6) detoxification/rehabilitation programs and (7) child care services.

Despite the availability of various resources, the staff encounters many difficulties in referring community resources to clients. First is the difficulty arising from the clients' reluctance and misconception about the resources as well as their great fluctuation in their abilities to perform A.D.L. (activities of daily living). Within the Medical Social Work Department, the difficulties come from the limited information about the available resources and its inadequacy for present use.

From the intra- and inter-organizational level, unclear referral criteria and service boundaries are pointed out. The coordination and feedback system on case development are poor. Throughout the referring process, the staff come across long waiting lists before clients are to be arranged for the needy resources. Furthermore, the process from application to final reply is long and there is no exception or flexibility for urgent cases.

To cope with the problems in the present resources networking, suggestions are invited. Internally, to adopt the concept of case management and its model and to set up a clear guideline in serving the elderly clients are suggested. It is hoped to update and enrich the various resources information. Practical support like clerical support and telephone system are advised. Besides, the clients' own resources can be developed through forming self-help groups or utilizing the patient resources centre.

At intra- and inter-organizational levels, clear referral criteria and division of labor are proposed. Improved mutual communication and cooperation through visits, coordinating meeting, conference and flexibility in policies are suggested so that urgent cases can be taken into consideration and resources can be best utilized. A channel for the feedback system of case development can be made use through memo, reply letter or indirect contacts. The need to bridge the service gap among social services agencies is also highlighted.

The need to act upon the suggestions and the applicability of case management model is acknowledged. An operational manual is to be drafted for handling elderly cases.

Operational Manual for Handling Elderly (Aged 60+) Cases

Rationale

a) There is a pressing request for ensuring a good quality of service through standardization of its service delivery system.
b) Elderly clients are chosen as the target of the first operational manual because of their representativeness: they are admitted to various wards, except Paediatric and Mentally Handicapped wards with different health problems representing over 60% of the total caseload.

Objectives

a) To suggest a framework of analysis such as the eco-map in order to have an overview on the needs and problems of the elderly clients.
b) To serve as a guideline or reminder aiming at fulfilling the "continuum of care" for patients from hospital to the community.
c) To compile a resources file with up-dated and comprehensive information for front-line staff's quick reference.

Target group

a) Elderly clients aged 60 or over.
b) They may either be in-patients, day-patients or out-patients of the hospital.

Screening criteria: To identify high psycho-social risk for elderly social work intervention

a) Indicators for stressful social situation

    (1)   aged 70 or over
    (2)   living alone
    (3)   with no accompanied relative or friend
    (4)   no discernible social support
    (5)   no fixed abode
    (6)   unknown case
    (7)   abused or neglected
    (8)   undergone family violence
    (9)   suicidal
    (10)   alcoholic and/or drug addict

b) Indicators from health problems which make an impact on clients' social functioning

    (11)   severity of illness: life threatening, e.g. carcinoma
    (12)   severity of illness: physical dysfunctional, e.g. CVA
    (13)   chronic illness, e.g. COAD
    (14)   mental dysfunction, e.g. dementia
    (15)   expected length of stay: 14 days or over
    (16)   unclear post hospital plan
    (17)   re-admitted to hospital within 30 days of discharge and without a medical reason

Referral criteria

Clients indicated with at least two of the above characteristics are recommended to be referred to early social work intervention.

Assessment

a) The principles

> (1) Physical, psychological and social factors are closely inter-related. Their dynamic interactions should be looked into carefully. Thus, frequent and close contact with the multi-disciplinary team members is strongly recommended for better understanding of clients' conditions.
>
> (2) The assessment framework merely serves as a reminder or guideline in the assessment process. Social work input and professional judgment on the uniqueness of individual case is definitely necessary.
>
> (3) The assessment leads to the evaluation on clients' internal and external resources, and the implications for their needs and problems. Intervention strategies rely heavily on professional judgment and availability of community resources.
>
> (4) Clients' self-determination in formulating the immediate and long-term welfare plans is necessary before the service goals could be attained in an effective and efficient way.

b) The psycho-social-physical assessment

It provides an overview on the dynamic interaction among clients' physical, psychological and social needs and problems. Its purpose is to look for the tangible and intangible resources needed to attain the "total patient care" and also to set short-term and long-term goals in arranging the continuity of care.

c) The feature of the core tasks in assessment
d) The tool: to use eco-maps (Appendix IV) to have an overview on clients' needs and problems

Goal setting through using a verbal or written service agreement

a) List the objectives as reviewed by the patient, his/her family, physical and other medical or allied health staff.
b) Set up immediate and long term goals in the service agreement.

c) Identify the tasks for goal attainment and discuss them with patient, his/her family and other related bodies.

Implementation of the welfare plan

a) Counsel patient and/or his family regarding the adjustment to illness, change in life-style and the need for long term care.
b) Assist patient and/or family in setting up the service goals and evaluating the feasibility of their post-hospital plan.
c) Make recommendations to patient regarding the appropriate community resources needed.
d) Carry out the tasks according to the priority set:
   i) Identify appropriate community agency and make referral.
   ii) Engage in brief intermittent or on-going treatment with family members needing assistance.
e) Evaluate the results and the need for any modification

Unexpected complications

a) Change in medical condition of the client that the previous plan has to be altered.
b) Patient's and/or family's refusal for service.
c) Family's uncooperativeness in making plans, resistance to discharge, refusal to participate in the arrangement.
d) Patient is discharged before he/she is able to be seen by MSW.

Criteria for termination

a) The goal is achieved and patient's family appears stable in coping.
b) Goals cannot be achieved.
c) The patient refuses social work service.
d) The patient discharges against medical advice.
e) Death of the patient.
f) Medical treatment transfers to elsewhere.

Resources File

Objectives

To ensure individual staff an up-dated and brief information about the available community resources for their quick reference, and to facilitate the use of resources.

Characteristics

The file consists of referral criteria, target group, referral procedure as well as the telephone number of the contact person so that resources can be used conveniently.

Table of Content

a) Resources for home care services

    i)   community escort service
    ii)   day care centers
    iii)   family aid service
    iv)   geriatric day hospital
    v)   home help services
    vi)   respite care service

b) Resources for institutional care services

    i)   private nursing homes registered in the SWD
    ii)   subvented aged homes and Care and Attention Homes
    iii)   infirmary service

c) Resources for financial assistance

    i)   comprehensive social security scheme
    ii)   funding

d) Resources for housing/accommodation

    i)   temporary shelters
    ii)   permanent placement

e) Resources for social follow up services

    i)   counseling services in FCSs

    ii)   therapeutic treatment/rehabilitation programmes

Implications of the Implementation of Case Management Model

The service delivery system

The modification of the service delivery system through implementing the case management model, "one of social work's core technologies" (Dant and Gearing, 1990, p. 331), helps to add the strength in the MSWD. This comprehensive, effective and efficient way of handling clients' problems ensures a full coverage of clients' welfare plan and the quality of service can also be guaranteed.

Intra-organizational collaboration

The hospital as a multi-disciplinary setting implies that none can do their job well alone. Intra-organizational collaboration is necessary. Medical social workers can state clearly their services through sharing their operational manual with other allied health professionals, which aim at not being involved in intra-organizational conflicts throughout the restructuring process of the Hospital Authority. With a clear presentation of the service delivery system, it allows the multi-disciplinary team to understand the approach the medical social workers adopt, the perspective they use to look into clients' needs and problems, and also the strategies used to formulate a welfare plan. But still, it allows room for social work assessment and professional judgment. Only the mutual understanding and cooperative attitude among the different professions can the ideal of "total patient care" be achieved.

Inter-organizational linkage

The fragmented resources can be coordinated better through a close linkage among the social welfare agencies. Nevertheless, the administrative loopholes have to be dealt with before the welfare plan can be achieved, especially their referring criteria and procedure. The case management model emphasizes on both formal and informal networking. Realization of community care can only be done through inter-organizational cooperation. The formal relationship is governed by their rules and regulations, but the informal one can be enhanced through their same orientation for clients' welfare. Though there is no one who is formally appointed as the case manager or resources coordinator, there is still a need to have somebody to ensure the attainment of clients' care plan. Medical social workers are used to assuming this role and provide a comprehensive service package for their clients. That is why they value much the inter-organizational cooperation and its function in facilitating an efficient and effective service delivery.

Conclusion

With a growth in the number of social services available to support the practical realization of "community care" and the recent expansion of a comprehensive hospital services aimed at providing "total patient care", the traditional medical social service is outdated. A systematic framework and procedure for operation is cried for. Though there is no one single best way to solve the present administrative problems, the case management model is examined as a useful conceptual framework as well as procedure for daily practice. Although there is no one best way to handle cases, its ability to serve medical-social goals cannot be neglected. Its focus on the vulnerable groups such as the elderly or handicapped and its emphasis on resources networking do certainly complement the medical social work practice. It suggests the need to look for a comprehensive service package so as to have an effective and efficient service provision. It fulfills the present need for a hospital based system of coordinating care through case management and enable MSWD to face the climate of quality assurance and the policy of cost-effectiveness/ cost containment. The re-organization of the service delivery system starts with the elderly clients, and the consolidation of intra- and inter-organizational relationships hopes to shed light on future continuous evaluation on the professional practice and the intra- and inter-organization connections.

Case management may be a new trend for coordinating the fragmented social service in Hong Kong. However, none is formally appointed as the "keyworker" or assumes the role as case manager. To oversee the various social services, it is hoped that the Hong Kong Council of Social Services will take up the role in coordinating case management in various types of social services and different clients so as to have cost-effectiveness in using the available resources.

References

Austin, Coral D (1990) "Case management: Myths and realities", *Families in Society,* Vol.17.

Ballew and Mink (1986) *Case Management in the Human Services.* Charles C Thomas Publisher.

Cambridge, Paul (1993) "Case management in community services: Organizational responses", *British Journal of Social Work,* Vol. 22.

Dant, Tim and Gearing, Brian (1990) "Key workers for elderly people in the community: Case managers and care coordinators", *Journal of Social Work* Vol. 19.

Hasenfeld, Yeheskel (ed) (1989) *Administrative Leadership in Social Services: The Next Challenge.* Haworth Press.

Huxley, Peter (1993) "Case management and care management in community care", *British Journal of Social Work*, Vol. 23.

Marsha Mailick Seltzer and Associates (1992) "Professional and family collaboration in case management: A hospital based replication of a community-based study" *Social Work in Health Care: A Quarterly Journal,* Vol. 17, No.1.

Moore, Stephen T (1990) "A social work practice model of case management: The case management grid", *Social Work.*

Morore, Stephen (1992) "Case management and the integration of service delivery systems shape case management", *Social Work.*

Netting, F. Ellen (1990) "Case management: Services or symptom?" *Families in Society,* Vol.17.

Rothman, Jack (1991) "A model of case management: Towards empirically based practice", *Social Work.*

Toba Schwaber Kerson and Associates (1989) *Social Work in Health Settings.* Haworth Press.

Appendix I

Stages of Case Management

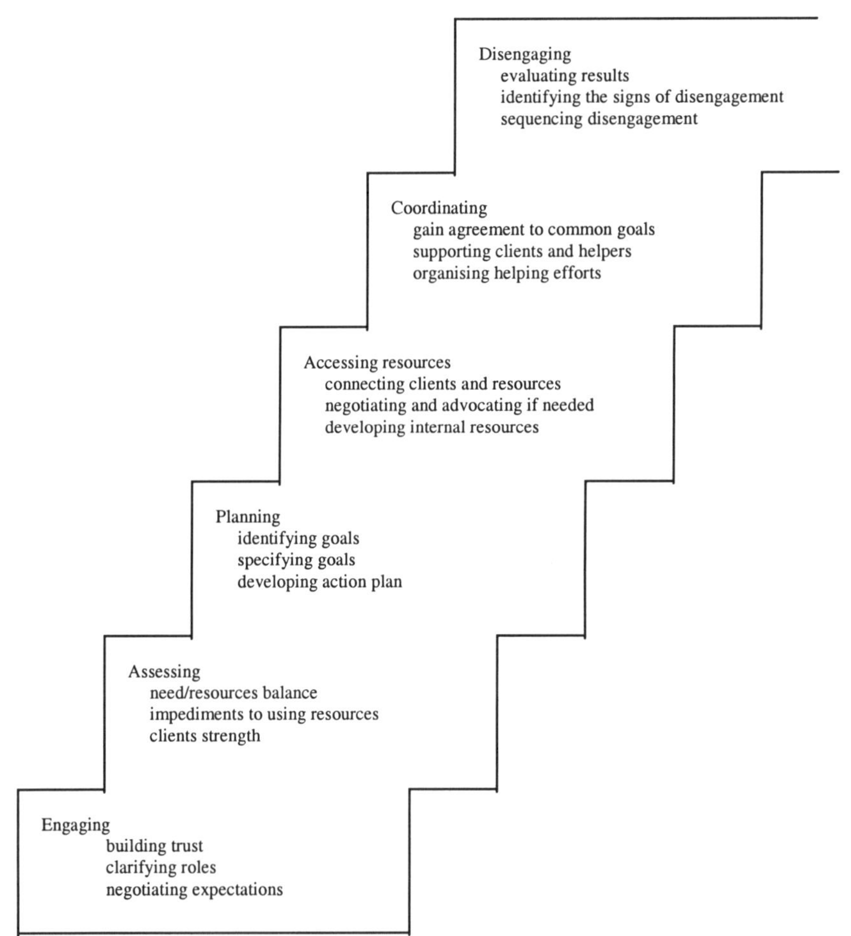

Source: Ballew and Mink, 1986, p. 11

Appendix II

Process of Case Management Model

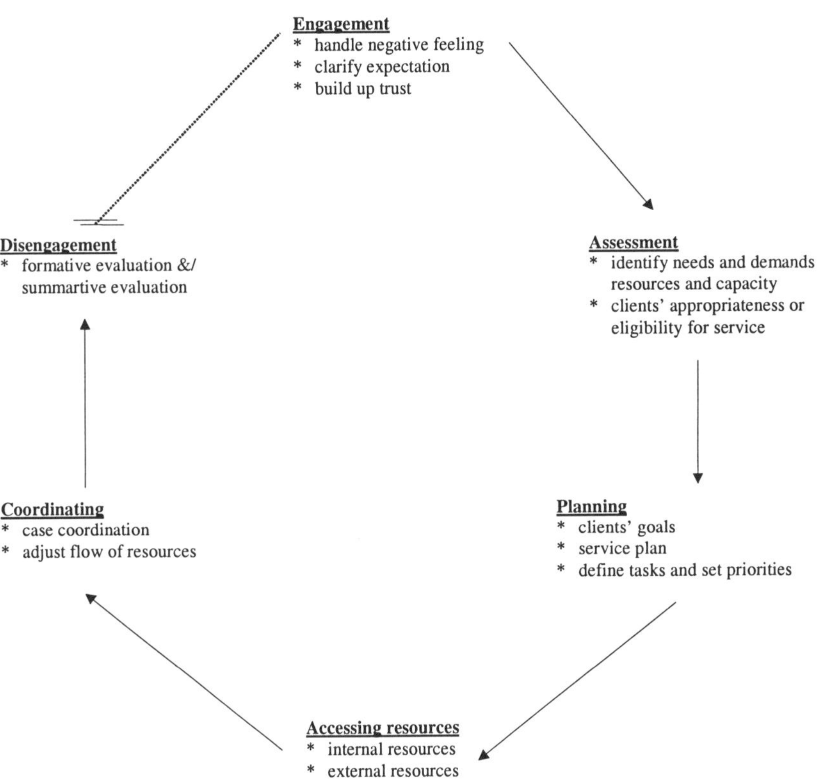

Appendix III

Case Management Process (modified) in Medical Social Work Department

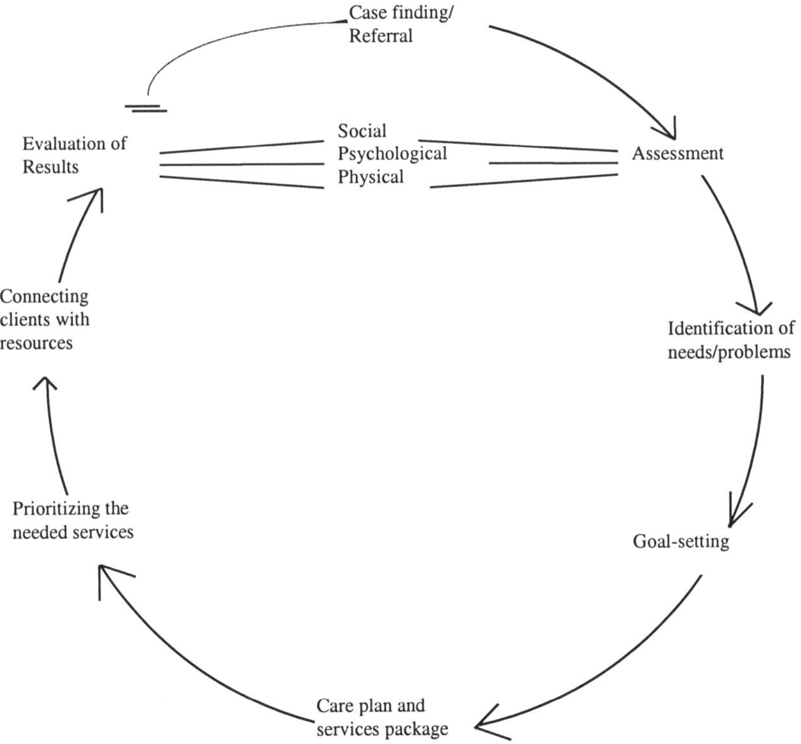

Appendix IV

ECOMAP

(*Please use this eco-map when the quality of a client's transactions with major elements in his environment is needed to be shown.)

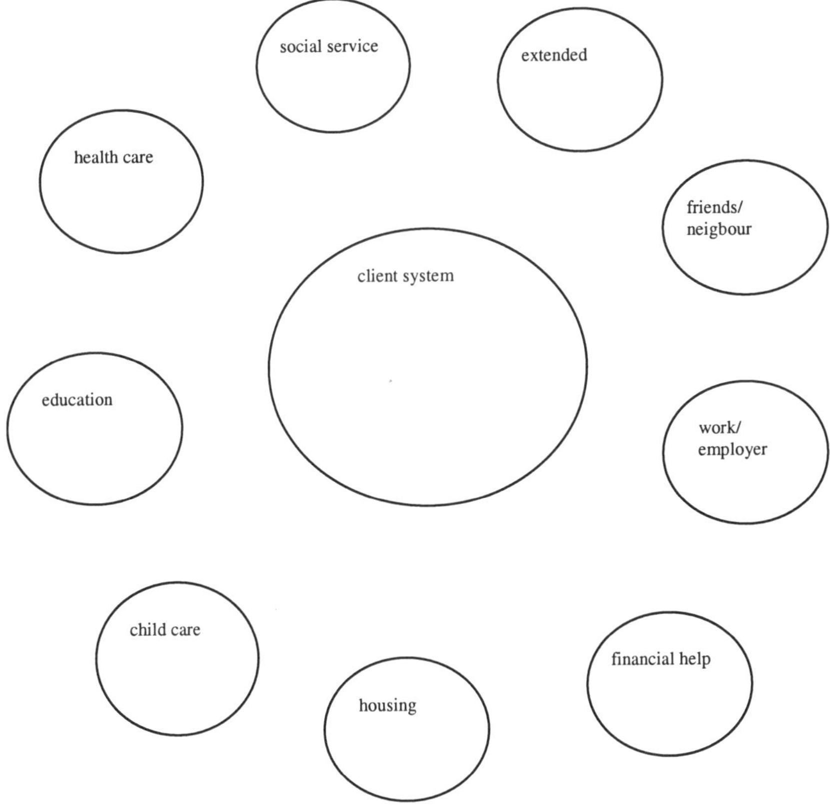

*—— strong

—— tenuous

///// stressful

* arrow along lines for the flow of energy and resources

——► away from client

◄—— towards client

Appendix V

Psycho-Social-Physical Assessment

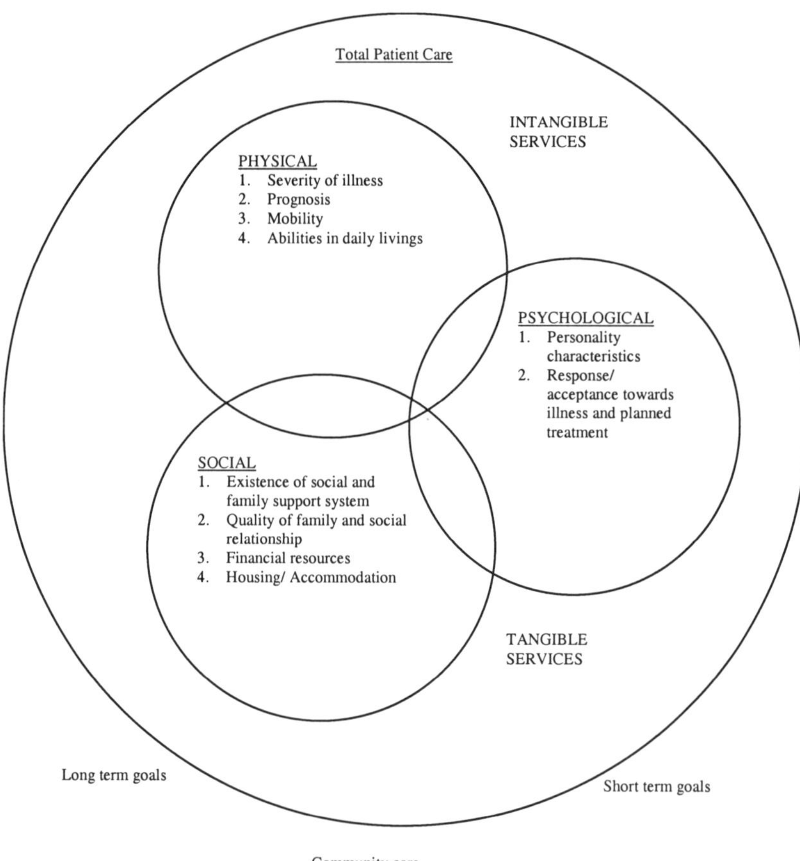

Appendix VI

The Feature of Core Tasks in Case Management

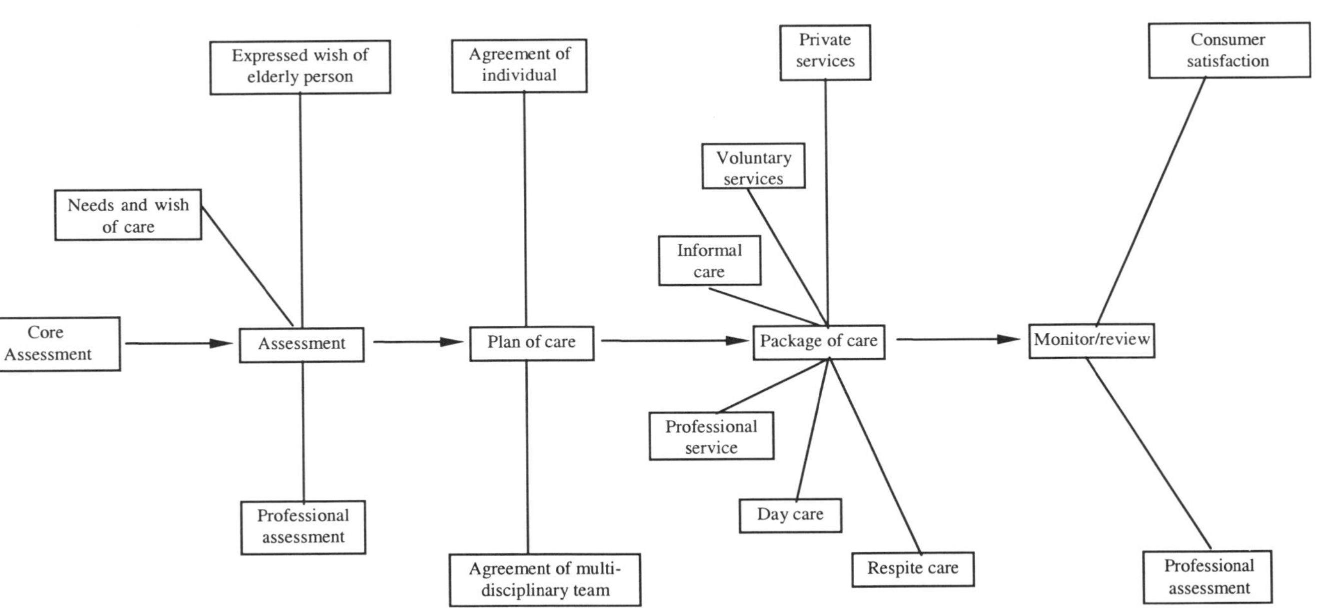

Source: Tim Dant and Brian Gearing, 1990, p. 337

8

Customer Participation in Management Reform: Examples from Medical Social Service Settings

Zarina C.L. LAM

Background

Health care reform of hospital service in the 1990s has defined new directions and values which asked for new initiatives to achieve new targets within the management system. The newest vision set by the Hong Kong Hospital Authority for the Year 2000 is the establishment of a seamless health care system, through which a collaborative effort between community health care providers and the hospitals can maximize patient service in servicing patients and families in Hong Kong (The Hong Kong Hospital Authority, 1993–1995). With an integral strategy to link up hospital and the community carers, promoting participation from different sectors to contribute in the quality patient service delivery became inevitable.

Enhancing participation of the health care providers within a rapidly changing and high technological health care system implies that the health care teams will inform the other parties with their current expertise. The increasing expectations from community on different dimensions of quality requires feedback from the users who can provides guidelines to prioritize the reform activities. The changing population which involves delivery of long term care to an aging group or people with chronic disability would require more attention to the family carers and other supporters in the community. Nonetheless, direct participation of patients and their satisfaction in the service quality will be regarded as the most important components in the reform process (Clemenhagen, 1994; Rosenau, 1994; Williams, 1994).

This paper will discuss how medical social service, as one of the many health care providers within a hospital setting, contributes to the corporate management reform which is somewhat different from the traditional human service delivery model. Some examples which the writer had participated at different extent in local and overseas situations will be used in this paper. The three illustrations will demonstrate efforts of social workers in promoting participation of internal and external customers and collecting feedback through a satisfaction study.

Customer Participation in Corporate Model

Customers of medical social service are defined as the users of medical social service department. As the medical social service department is located inside a hospital, hospital users can therefore, become customers of the department. For example, patients and families who are undergoing treatment or providing escort to hospital are potential customers of the medical social service department. There are other people who work or have transaction with the medical social service, i.e., hospital staff who need information or send referrals to medical social service for various reasons are users and customers of the department (Chaston, 1994).

Therefore customers are categorized into four major groups, namely internal, external, direct or indirect users. The internal customers are staff from different health care professionals and non-professionals. The external customers include people and ex-patients (Fig. 1).

1) Patients & families
2) Hospital staff
3) Professionals and training institutes
4) The community and the public

Internal	External
In-patients/Out-patients & families	Ex-patients
staff	volunteer
	training institutes
	community service organizations
	media
	public

Degrees of participation

There will be at least four different levels or modes of participation of health care customers occurring in the management reform process. The extent of participation ranged from a minimal extent, e.g., giving informal opinions, to the more involved in the improvement process and full participation which result in some action in the change process.

1) To provide immediate feedback as a means to ask for improvements or give recognition to a satisfactory service outcome
2) To advocate for changes with direct focus on area(s) for improvement
3) To be involved in system planning and decision-making
4) To provide additional resources or initiate new efforts for problem prevention or service promotion

minimal

Opinions	Versus	Actions
Informal verbal recognition or complainants		Peer advocate
Written feedback media		Pressure
Advisory member		Management board
Feedback study on user satisfaction		Volunteers agency
collaboration		

full participation

Some Examples on Customer Participation in Health Care Management Reform

1. Internal change through interdisciplinary team feedback

The daily work of a medical social work department usually has its reliance on collaborative efforts from multi-disciplinary teamwork. Serving patients and families in a Canadian hospital in early the 1990s has allowed the writer of this paper to have first-hand experience in establishing quality standards through internal customer feedback study.

Four areas of feedback were perceived as very important to social work as part of a multi-disciplinary team in serving patients and their families.

1.1 Effectiveness on hospital social service
1. responsiveness to patient/family needs
2. timely psychosocial assessments and information to other team member in planning for intervention
3. improvement in the patient and/or family adjustment to hospitalization if needed
4. carrying out the intervention plan as stated
5. linkage of patient and/or family with access community resources

1.2 As a member of a hospital staff team
1. participates effectively in patient care rounds
2. co-ordinates discharge plan effectively
3. utilizes knowledge on psychosocial care and community resources to assist in developing a discharge plan
4. communicates effectively with team members regarding patient situation and progress on a day to day basis (verbal and written)
5. readily available to respond to crisis situations
6. able to identify and respond to the changing needs of the patient population and the unit
7. demonstrates an ability to function effectively under increasing demands

1.3 Providing administrative support in hospital environment
1. demonstrates knowledge of hospital policies and procedures
2. discusses with patients in a respectful and dignified manner

1.4 Feedback on departmental performance
1. cover adequate areas of social work
2. responds sufficiently to changing hospital needs
3. be involved in hospital wide education
4. be involved in the provision of patients service

Most health care team members cherished this opportunity to give feedback and they were impressed with the idea that not only were they invited to become customers of the service but also they could give opinions in the departmental improvement process.

2. Patient satisfaction and feedback

A local pilot study on patient satisfaction was conducted in 1994. Patients' feedback on hospitalization was surveyed. The writer was involved in planning for the project as well as the implementation of the study. Social worker' inputs were important because of the nature of service delivery. For instance, a patient-centred approach was adopted in social work practice and the perception of a "patient", in many situations has its significance in balancing "organic" or "disease" perspective in the design of the questionnaire. Medical social work were also involved in many hospitalization procedures which require feedback from the customers of hospital. In the patient satisfaction study, both hospital service procedures and personal preferences were studied.

2.1 Hospital service delivery
1. admission time, information, customer service and assistance
2. professional services in ward
3. general patient support and communication pattern in ward
4. discharge time, information, customer and assistance

2.2 Physical environment
   1. atmosphere, space and greenery
   2. patients' choices: clothes, food
   3. entertainment or drop-in areas

Data from a pilot patient feedback could provide reference on the service standard. To establish a continuous improvement process, baseline measures allowed service comparisons too. Medical social workers did provide a significant contribution to train research assistant or recruit qualified volunteers in the study.

3. *Facilitating change action through new community and patient resource center: An interface between service providers and active customers*

The writer had also participated as an advisor to the new patient service model in Hong Kong between 1993–1996. It was then that a new patient service was highly emphasized for achieving a total care mission. Each year, a few hospital-based patient resource centers became in use. Some experience will be discussed below.

With the "hospital without wall" slogan introduced in the early 1990s in local hospitals, the public and local community who require health care information or services became customers of a hospital. The establishment of a new patient resource center in major hospitals brings some social workers to a medical setting. The patient center provides a physical space for patients to meet and share experience with one another. The sharing of patients who have different hospital and treatment experiences when expressed can easily be channeled into action.

3.1 Total patient care service provision
   1. provides information and resources on health and disease
   2. promotes self help and mutual help spirit
   3. fosters a positive attitude in the community
   4. facilitates community participation in establishing a supportive network which address the needs of patients

5. co-ordinates hospital resources to meet community needs, e.g., community health education and prevention activities
6. provides social service networking and patients' referrals to social service organizations

3.2 Facilitating active participation
   1. co-ordinates and facilitates volunteer service
   2. provides community-based resource liaison and mobilization

Customers' efforts are facilitated through this interface between the hospital and the community. Social workers' roles in co-ordinating hospital staff or ex-patients as volunteers to serve patients, answering enquiries and accumulating information into patient resource files were well recognized as new and essential in improving patient service quality. The public and many community organizations are no longer passive external customers but are now participants who can contribute to the new health care management system.

Discussions

From the last few years' experience, it could be generally concluded that the process of enhancing customer participation might go through different entry points depends on each context. Two examples of soliciting ideas and opinions for improvement in service implementation from both internal customers, i.e., patients and staffs, were discussed. There are, however, other feedback study from the external customers, for instance, obtaining feedback from the volunteers, public representatives from training institutions, and other users of hospital services through formal and informal channels.

The new management paradigm which empowers customers to understand the service delivery by information and other educational material, to further involve actions for improvement was illustrated by a new community and patient resource center structure. With participation of staff and patient groups, a new service mode became possible in meeting more aspects of patients' needs. Hospital effectiveness is thus seen as extending itself into the community and preventive levels. It is only by getting opinions from customers on what they desire and putting the needs into changed action that are feasible and manageable that the ultimate objective of improvement can be materialized.

Finally, with a well established and build-in system of monitoring feedback, encouragement on participation, support and information to empower customers' level of participation, a community can enjoy a better health environment (Taylor R., 1984; Rousseau, C., 1993; Labonte, R., 1994 and Cowger, C., 1994).

Conclusion

The importance of continuous and collaborative effort was observed within the last few years by the writer's participation in the process of health care management reform'. It was learnt from the experience that internal and external customers should be seen as both sides of a coin which contributes and grows at the time within a new health care system for a reform that the impacts on quality service came forth. There were some other cultural factors on patients' readiness to express opinions. For example, many elderly people are very modest and reserved in giving critical feedback. Efforts to enhance their expressiveness through non-verbal means, such as expressive artwork and informal focus group sharing had proved to be effective (Jones, D. and Lester, C., 1994; Tower K., 1994).

To conclude, social work's expertise in human service delivery and efforts in enhancing participation of internal (patients, families, staff) and external (ex-patients or volunteer, non-government organizations, public) customers in health care management reform should also be well recognized.

References

An interdisciplinary staff feedback study. Medical social work department, The Riverdale Hospital, Toronto, Ontario. (unpublished)

Chang, F. & Chan, C. (1994) Alternative social work intervention approaches in hospital setting-patient resource center. A chapter in Community Development Resource Book, Hong Kong Council of Social Service.

Chaston, I. (1994) A comparative study of internal customer management practices within service sector firms and the National Health Service. *Journal of Advanced Nursing*, **19**(2) 299–308.

Clemenhagen, C. (1994) Patient satisfaction: The power of an untapped resource. *Canadian Medical Association Journal*, **150**(11), 1771–1772.

Cowger C. (1994) Assessing client strengths: Clinical assessment for client empowerment. *Social work*, **39**(3), 262–268.

Everett, B. & Boydell, K. (1994) A methodology for including consumers' opinions in mental health evaluation research. *Hospital Community Psychiatry*, **45**(1), 76–78.

Jones, D. & Lester, C. (1994) Hospital care and discharge: Patients' and carers' opinions. *Age Aging*, **23**(2), 91–96.

Labonte R. (1994) Health promotion and empowerment: Reflections on professional practice. *Health Education Quarterly*, **21**(2), 253–268.

Report on Pilot Survey on Patient Feedback and Satisfaction (1994) Department of Applied Social Studies, Hong Kong Polytechnic University.

Rosenau, P. (1994) Health Politics meets post–modernism: Its meaning and implications for community health organising. *Journal of Health, Politics, Policy, Law*, **19**(2), 303–333.

Rousseau, C. (1993) Community empowerment: The alternative resources movement in Quebec. *Community Mental Health Journal*, **29**(6), 535–546.

Stevens, M. Curl, R. & Rule, S. (1993) From Protection to independence: Utilising intersector co-operation to ensure consumer options. *Journal of Rehabilitation*, **59**(1), 35–39.

Taylor, R. (1984) Friends can be good medicine: An excursion into mental health promotion. *Community Mental Health Journal*, **20**(4), 294–303.

The Hong Kong Hospital Authority Business Plans 1993/94 to 4/1995.

The Pamela Poude Nethersole Eastern Hospital, Patient and Community Resource Center. Organisational objectives. Internal document.

Tower, K. (1994) Consumer-centered social work practice: Restoring client self-determination. *Social work*, **39**(2), 191–196.

Williams, B. (1994) Patient satisfaction: A valid concept? *Social Science and Medicine*, **38**(4) 509–516.

Williams, D. (1991) Policy at the grassroots: Community-based participation in health care policy. *Journal of professional nursing*, **7**(5): 271–276.

Wong, R. (1989) Community participation in primary health care. *Hong Kong Nursing Journal*, **47**, 10–11.

9

Establishment of a Computerized Management Information System in a Social Welfare Agency: A Case Illustration

AU Wai Cheung, Cliff

Introduction

Traditionally, management activities include planning, budgeting, coordinating, controlling, staffing, etc. What makes these activities possible and effective is information. According to Mintzberg's (1975) study, there are three main groups of managerial roles that a manager has to play in his or her daily work routine. They are the interpersonal roles, informational roles and decisional roles. The informational roles of a manager, requires responsibility for receiving and transmitting information internally as well as externally. Mintzberg describes the informational functions of a manager as the "nerve centre" of an organization. It is because a manager is in the key position of the information flow of an agency.

There is no exception in social welfare agency . It needs information to link up all the management activities to achieve organizational goals. According to Chan's (1992) empirical study, Information Processing was ranked first in occupying the working time of first-line administrators of the social welfare administration in Hong Kong. It means that effective social welfare administrators should be able to reach and process information. Service information is essential for many administrative tasks such as decision making, organization, coordinating, budgeting, planning and evaluating, etc. Mastering of a large bundle of information becomes the crux of any accountable and efficient service delivery today. For instance, it is impossible to have a realistic service plan and budgeting without the information of a clientele and agency's resources flow. Management Information System (MIS) has been an important topic for modern business organizations for decades. Though there are numerous information systems in the social welfare agency such as clientele information, payroll, accounting and service statistics, etc., MIS is still a strange term for human service personnel. However, administrators of social service agencies are enhancing their awareness to the importance of information systems in performing their managerial roles. Social service administrators often fail to perform duties effectively and efficiently because of a lack in inappropriate, timely and accurate information or incapability of information processing. Therefore, MIS is crucial for all social welfare administrators nowadays.

On the other hand, there is also an observable trend that the use of the computer is the common strategy of social welfare organizations to enhance their information processing efficiency. The Research Department of the Hong Kong Council of Social Services (HKCSS) (1993) completed a telephone survey of its member agencies on the use of the computer accounting package "Real World".

Table 1. The use of computer of social welfare agencies in Hong Kong (extracted and adapted from *Welfare Digest*, 93–11).

Computer Use Items or Situations	*Percentage*
Agencies adopting word processing packages	73.5%
Agencies using accounting packages	59.8%
Agencies adopting data analysis packages	50.0%
Non-computerized agencies going to be computerized	43.3%
Sample size = 132 agencies	

The study results reflected that out of 132 responding member agencies, 59.8% (79 agencies) were using computer accounting packages and 43.4% (23 agencies) of non-computerized agencies were going to use one in future. Besides accounting packages, over 70% of the agencies were adopting word processing, whereas 50% were using data analysis software. The study also highlighted that the prevalent rate of computer use in social welfare agencies might be under represented for various reasons. The above findings to a certain extent reflected that the use of the computer is prevalent in Hong Kong social welfare agencies nowadays.

Recently, the Coordinating Committee on Children and Youth Centre of the HKCSS had also put the item of computerization into the agenda of its 3rd Meeting in 1994. The Committee reaffirmed the need of computerization for centre service data and invited the Information Science Department of a local university to offer technological assistance. This development implied that computers were the common office equipment in children and youth centres. Furthermore, computerized systems of children and youth centres in Hong Kong are developing on an inter-agencies level and advancing with a more standardized and coordinated pace. Therefore, it is worthwhile to study the significance of MIS and the use of the computer in order to build up references for those social welfare agencies that are going to computerize their information systems.

This article aims at introducing the implication of MIS and its relationship with the use of computer. The process of computerizing information system will also be illustrated with a local case study. Finally, some key issues in the process of computerization will also be discussed.

Management Information Systems

Information systems are vital to the operation and management of every modern organization. What then is information? A useful definition for information system can be drawn from Davis and Olson (1985: 200–201) who defined that "Information is data that has been processed into a form that is meaningful to the recipient and is of real or perceived value in current or prospective actions or decisions", and the term "data" refers to "groups of non-random symbols which represent quantities, actions, objects, etc.". The relation of data to information is that of raw material to the finished product. In other words, an information system processes data into information. Conceptually, information for one person may be raw data for another, because different levels of operation in an organization need different information. The information for frontline staff may only be raw data for supervisors and so on (vice versa). Furthermore, if there is no current or future choices or decisions (decision-making), information would be unnecessary or meaningless for the recipient. In short, information has value only when it can be a reference for users' decision or action to be taken.

Information is data that has been processed and is meaningful to a user. A system is a set of components that operate together to achieve a common purpose. A larger system comprises subsystems. "The system concept of MIS is therefore one of optimizing the output of the organization by connecting the operating subsystems through the medium of information exchange" (Murdick *et al.*, 1987, p. 6). With understanding of these two terms, MIS thus collects, transmits, processes, and stores data, and retrieves and distributes information to various users in an organization. "The objective of an MIS is to provide information for decision making on planning, initiating, organizing, and controlling the operations of the subsystems of the firm (or organization) and to provide a synergistic organization in the process" (Murdick *et al.*, 1987, p. 6). To elaborate on this definition, Head (1967, p. 23) described MIS as a pyramid (Fig. 1).

MIS
for
strategic
and policy
planning and
decision making

Management information
for tactical planning
and decision making

Management information for
operational planning, decision making
and control

Transaction processing
Inquiry response

Fig. 1. Management Information System.

The pyramid contains four layers. The bottom layer consists of information for transaction processing and inquiry responses; the next layer provides management information for operational planning, decision making and control, the third level contributes to information system resources in supporting tactical planning and decision making for management control, while the top level is the information support strategic planning for the whole organization by the highest levels of management.

Davis and Olson (1984, p. 6) went on to define MIS in a more comprehensive way that it "is an integrated, user-machine system for providing information to support operations, management, and decision-making functions in an organization. The system utilizes computer hardware and software; manual procedures; models for analysis, planning, control and decision making; and a database". There is always a confusion of the differences between computerization and development of MIS. An MIS, in fact, can exist without computers, but it is the power of the computer which makes MIS feasible. That is why Davis and Olson defined MIS as a user-machine system. The question is not whether computers should be used in MIS, but the extent to which information systems should be computerized. The concept of user-machine system implies that some tasks are best performed by humankind, while others are best done by machines.

Thus for a computerized information system to be deemed successful, its benefits to the user must outweigh its costs. The system must improve the performance of its users and be applicable to major problems of an organization. User satisfaction is always regarded as an indicator of a system's success. Therefore, Ahituv and Neumann (1990, pp. 6–7) summarized that a successful information system is "profitably applied to an area of major concern to the organization, is widely used by one or more satisfied managers, and improves the quality of their performance". Furthermore, they also listed many critical variables that achieves an information system's success. Such variables include user involvement, user attitudes and cognitive style, top-management support, budgets, user education and training, psychological climate in an organization, organizational maturity, resource availability, and organization size. All these variables, and many more, are important. Any single variable may lead to the failure of a system, but no variable alone determines success. The outcome is usually the result of a complex interplay among the variables that determine the starting point, the development process, and the resulting system. A unique combination of variables is peculiar to each organization. Therefore, "an information system cannot be brought off the shelf. It must be tailored to the organization — to its management, the users and implementers of the information system, the resources and the technology available" (Ahituv and Neumann, 1990, pp. 6–7).

Every organization, to a certain extent, operates in a peculiar way. An agency tends to establish its own approaches of data collection and information processing. Since the investment on development of a computerized information system and the installation of hardware and software are expensive, more reliance on the experience of other agencies should be considered. This paper is going to present the computerization process of a single-service centre based agency in Hong Kong. With the illustration of this case, we can consolidate the experience which may be a reference for other human service organizations in computerizing their own information systems.

Computerization of the *Friends of Scouting*: A Case Illustration

Background of organization

The Friends of Scouting (FOS) is a subsidiary of the Scout Association of Hong Kong. It is fully subsidized by the Social Welfare Department of the Hong Kong Government. The service domain of the organization involves children and youth centre services. Under the headquarter of the FOS, there are a total of eight centre service units including two youth centres, one children centre and five children and youth centres located in various districts. Up to 31 March 1995, there were altogether about 55 program staff serving 9667 members in these centres. As the organization grows, administration work and information (information overload?) needed to be handled become bulky and complex. While the FOS is a comparatively small agency that is not eligible to have financial support from the government for its central administration personnel expenses, more and more administration and accounting work are shifted to centre staff. As a result, manpower input to direct service delivery is affected as some manpower were deployed to handle the administration and accounting work.

On the other hand, there is a growing demand for stricter accountability for social service administrators. The government becomes more critical to the performance and effectiveness of the social welfare agencies. As a matter of fact, social service agencies have no landed right to be ineffective or to fail to evaluate the productivity of their working approaches. In early 1992, the establishment of the working party on The Review of The Children and Youth Centre Services (1994) was the response to this critique. The orientation of this Working Party was to review the existing service delivery model and structure of children and youth centres in order to ensure that the service policy objectives are being effectively achieved.

In short, accountability has become a popular word in the social service field nowadays. In the hope of handling the daily and routine job duties effectively and improving the mechanism of service accountability, computerization was initiated by the social work officer) (SWO) who is the supervisor of all the FOS centres . Following to this initiation, a Working Group on computerization was formed in September, 1988.

Computerization Working Group

Since there was a complaint from centre staff about overloaded administration work besides their daily direct services, the SWO initiated a proposal to computerize the agency's information systems in a Centre-in-Charge (CIC) meeting . With the promise to improve the situation of overloaded administration work, a Working Group on Computerization was formed.

The working group was constituted with SWO, executive officers of headquarters and three CICs. Since computers were not a subvention item, funding sources and technical support of computerization could only depend on the agency's capacity. From the very beginning, none of the working group members knew much about computerization or even the computer. What they could do was to learn from the experiences of other computerized social welfare agencies while some of the group members started to explore and study any suitable software and hardware for the computerization.

The working group has lasted for seven years. It shifted from an *ad hoc* working group to a standing working group in the organization structure. Such a status change is a recognition of the agency for its commitment to computerization. Since the involvement of group members, especially the three CICs, was mainly out of personal interest, the members spend a lot of private time and extra effort in studying the process of computerization and testing the developed system.

However, the agency expected the working group to perform several functions including:

1. To plan and initiate a comprehensive procedure for agency computerization.
2. To implement computerization in various centres of the agency such as system analysis, developing application software and operation manual, etc.
3. To coordinate and evaluate the process of computerization in every centre, and
4. To provide training and technical support for all relevant staff of the centres.

According to the consensus from the CIC meeting, the objectives of the agency computerization were:

1. To improve the efficiency of data processing and information management in every centre of FOS.
2. To ameliorate staff efficiency with the help of the computer in service delivery, and
3. To enhance the effectiveness of service evaluation and analysis so that more accurate program and service data and statistics can be provided for government and sponsoring authorities.

Progress of Computerization in FOS

Seven years after the launching of computerization, the progress of the computerization can be summarised in the following:

Period	Task Completed
Sept 1988	• Working group formed • Starting point of computerization identified • Two centres assigned as testing centres (one is single and one is combined) in which CICs were members of the working group
End of 1988	• Two sets of 80 286 computers and nine-pin dot-matrix printers purchased for the testing centres • A Chinese database software adopted as the common application software for the development of various information systems
1989	• "Membership System" developed for membership records and was tested in the testing centres. The test lasted for one year and the system was proved to be reliable. This system could also process membership information reports for agencies, the HKCSS and Social Welfare Department.
1990	• Six sets of 80 286 computers and 24-pin dot-matrix printers purchased for the other six centres • Operation manual and work flow design of membership system completed • Adoption of membership system started in all centres • Development of "Book Keeping System" and "Program code System" started. The Book Keeping system shared the data of Program Code system.
1991	• Training workshop provided on the operation of Membership Record System to all operation staff and CICs • All FOS centres were required to adopt this system and transform the manual system to a computer system within one year. • Book Keeping and Program Code systems tested in the testing centres

continued

Period	Task Completed
1992	• Book Keeping and Program Code Systems proved to be reliable • Training workshop for CICs and operation staff (mostly clerical assistants) provided. All centres were required to adopt the new computerized Book Keeping System and Program Code System. • Transformation of a computerized membership system completed in all centres. Pace of computerization accelerated with the help of former experiences. As a result, three computer systems were developed simultaneously including "Program Statistics", "Inventory Record" and "Part-time Instructor Payroll". The program statistics system would link up the data bases of the program code system. • Test of new systems proceeded in the testing centres. • Membership System revised. The improved version was developed to facilitate the membership record operation.
Apr. 1993	• Training workshop provided on the above four systems • Compulsory adoption of revised membership system and the program statistics system enforced, while the inventory system and part-time instructor payroll remained optional.
1993	• "Program Enrolment System" developed to link up program statistics subsystem, program code subsystem and membership subsystem • Data security design completed to keep computers from abuse and to ensure information confidentiality • Four sets of 80 486 DX2 66 computers and printers purchased for four centres to facilitate further computerization
1994	• Another four sets of 486 computers and printers purchased for the remaining centres • Development of program enrolment system hindered as a result of the possible modification of CIS form and the change of information needs by the HKCSS and Social Welfare Department respectively after the Centre Review

Discussion

Integrative Development and Distributive Application

The above summary of the computerization progress showed the long path of change in FOS. Such a slow development pace was mainly due to a lack of experience, resources and technological support. With a trial-and-error basis and the extra effort of the working group members, it becomes reasonable for the group to take seven years for the computerization.

To conceptualize the above progress, we can recall what Davis and Olson (1984) mentioned before. The MIS can be seen as a loose integration of organizational subsystems. FOS's computerization seemed to aim at integrating its clientele record subsystem, accounting subsystem and program statistics subsystem into the enrolment subsystem with computer technology. A MIS typically provides the basis for integration of organizational information processing. If there is no integrating process and mechanism, the individual subsystems may be inconsistent and incompatible. Data items may be specified differently and may not be compatible across applications. To avoid this, FOS strictly centralizes the tasks of computerization to the working group and a diverse information subsystem is developed under an overall information system plan.

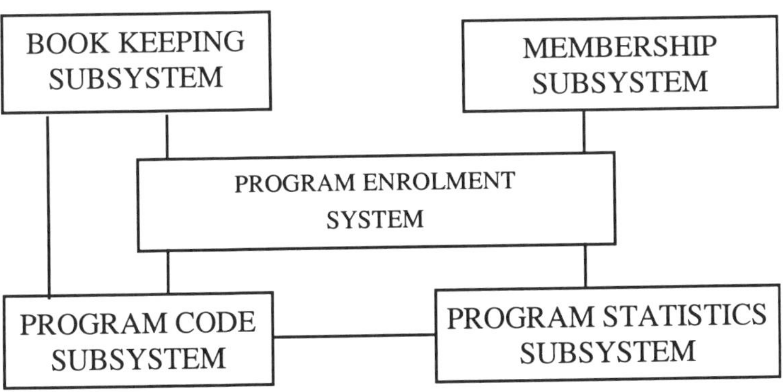

Fig. 2. Integrative Information System of FOS.

Let us review the FOS's computerization progress. We can identify that the development of the "Program Enrolment System" marks the completion of a specific stage of computerization in FOS. In other words, the stage goal of the FOS computerization was the installation of a comprehensive service information system that integrates the previously developed systems. The individual information subsystems were developed in sequence such that the antecedent system was developed to facilitate the following one for the sake of data transference, and was directed to the comprehensive integration system. Even though the information subsystems were implemented one at a time, the design could be guided by the overall direction, which determined how each of them fitted in with other subsystems. In the case of FOS, computerization was designed and progressed to be a planned federation of small subsystems. Furthermore, in-between the above computerization stages, many operation procedures and standards were also developed to assist the implementation of computerized systems. In addition, these standards, guidelines and procedures also achieved the integration of an information system.

Besides the approach of a centralized development of the integrated subsystems, the applications of the developed subsystems was decentralized to individual centres in FOS. This approach of decentralized application resulted in independent operation and separate data base in different centres. There was no common data base of all eight centres in the headquarters. The headquarters could only access the processed information reports from the centres rather than the raw data. Such an arrangement kept the FOS from additional computer work and allowed individual centres to have discretion in manpower deployment and computer operation for their unique situation. However, the coordination and monitoring of information systems became difficult for the FOS headquarters

The Choice of Information Systems (for computerization)

According to the idea of Tricker (1993), the scope of computerization depends on the extent to which information is codified and diffused. "Codified" refers to "information that can easily be set out on paper for transmission". "Diffused" means the "information that is readily shared"

(Tricker 1993, pp. 47–48). Computerization represents the application of computer rationality to data processing of specific shared tasks or information. In order for such specific tasks or information to be utilized by a computer, they have to be codified into binary logic with resultant reduction into bits of information. Therefore, only information or tasks that can be neatly categorized can be computerized (Murphy 1987).

High Codified and High Diffused Tasks (1)	High Codified and Low Diffused Tasks (2)
Low Codified and High Diffused Tasks (3)	Low Codified and Low Diffused Tasks (4)

Fig. 3. Typology of tasks adapted from Tricker (1993, p. 48).

Referring to the above typology, two extreme types of tasks or information can be identified. Type (4) task/information, which is low codified and low diffused, is best performed by human beings, while type (1) task/information that is high codified and high diffused, is best done by computers. Corresponding to the suggestions by Mutshler and Hoefer (1990), three factors affected the use of computer technology in a social welfare agency are whether specific tasks were structured, semi-structured or unstructured. The structured task seemed to be codified and diffused more easily than the unstructured task. Therefore, three different nature of tasks would affect the feasibility of the computerized system in different degrees.

In the case of FOS, the computerization started from membership record, accounting, and program information which were the most routine and repetitive task of children and youth centres. The data nature and the flow of these information were well-structured and analyzable or codifiable for computerization. In addition, membership record, financial flow and program statistics were the most important and widely shared information for program planning, begetting, evaluation and statistics of centre utilization for funding bodies. Furthermore, the accuracy of information was the most concerned issue of centre administrators. The computerization of membership record, accounting and program information systems can ensure support from the organization and enhancement of efficiency of information processing.

Strategies of Computerization

Reviewing the experience of FOS's computerization, there are some consolidations in the implementation strategies which are worthwhile to be mentioned here.

Firstly, the agency should establish a Computerization Process Framework before the implementation. The computerization process should include the identification of information needs for the user group, system analysis, program analysis and programming, training and implementation. As mentioned before, if there were no current or future choices or decision-making involved, information would be unnecessary or meaningless for the recipient. Information has value only as it affects the decision or action to be taken by the users. Determining where to start the computerization in an organization depends on the users' information needs for their daily duties and decision making. Users may include top management who needs information for strategic and policy planning, middle management who needs information for tactical planning and decision making, frontline supervisors who need information for operational control and frontline workers who need information to make inquiry response and transaction processing.

Once the information needs by specific users have been identified, the system analyst would study the organization thoroughly about data collection, information flow, requirement of hardware and software and personnel needed. Those study results form the system specifications for the next step of computerization. With the system specifications, the program analyst then transforms them into a computer program. He or she, corresponding to the system specification, suggests the program structure and works out the program specification for the computer programmer to finalize the application system for users.

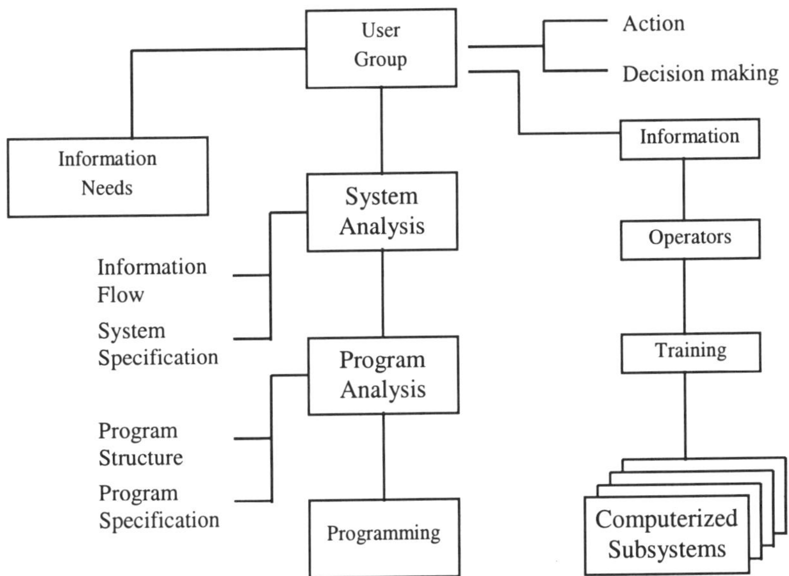

Fig. 4. Framework of computerization (extracted from Au 1995, p. 20).

In the case of FOS, the computerization process was based on this framework that the implementation was proceeded step by step. It was important to define the information needs and not needs for the centre staff and service and the areas that should be computerized. Once the computer information system has been developed, there would be a test run in the testing centres. After the effectiveness of the new system was affirmed, training for all relevant staff would follow. Finally, all centres would adopt the new system. The computerization process was implemented and monitored by the working group. Therefore, the working group members shared the roles of system developer, trainer and user. Such duplication of roles, on one hand diminished a communication blockage, but on the other hand overloaded and confused the working group members.

The second strategy is the standardization of equipment (hardware and software), operation procedures and data collection forms, etc. Basically, all the computerized information systems of FOS were developed from the same application computer software (the COMET 2, a powerful Chinese database software). This unity of application software enabled the transmission of data among various information subsystems. Besides, it also allowed the staff to master the computer commands and operation procedures more easily. Once they became familiar with any one of the information subsystems, they would have no problems handling the rest. In addition, the standardization of forms and operation made the coordination among centres feasible. The control and monitoring of centres' computer operation by the headquarters would also be possible.

The third strategy is the systemic documentation of computerization materials. Though sufficient technical support and resources supply are some of the major factors to safeguard the progress of computerization, the staff turn-over (especially the working group members) always affects the advancement of computerization in an organization. There are many examples that computerization developed by agency staff became an orphan and stopped to be further developed when relevant staff left the organization. To avoid this , the working group of FOS had tried hard to keep all the documents of the system specification and program specification of the developed information systems. Furthermore, operation manuals of every information system have also been written down and stored for the operation staff. A well established documentation system can ensure progress and make the follow-up of computerized systems possible.

The fourth strategy is the provision of necessary facilities and technical support throughout the computerization. This strategy is important in the beginning stage and for the maintenance of computerization. Since the installation of a computerized information system is a new attempt for the centres, securing the confidence of centre staff is the crux of success of the system. Appropriate and on-going in-service training and technical support are necessary to involve staff in the process of computerization. In the case of FOS, the working group also provided technical support to all centres. Immediate response and solution to the centres' requests on fixing computer problems was also important to maintain centre staff's motivation and confidence in using computerized information systems. Furthermore, the computerization is a long term investment of the organization. Periodical revision and evaluation about the operation, the equipment and information system is necessary to keep all centres remain flexible to react to changing needs.

Case Summary

The above case illustration about the computerization of FOS is actually a practical example of developing MIS in a social welfare agency. It has highlighted the background of the computerization that a more efficient and accurate handling of centre information might counter with external pressure on service effectiveness and accountability. Since the social welfare agency does not have enough resources support for computerization, the computerization process was administered by agency staff rather than external computer professionals. The formation of a responsible working group is one of the most common ways to computerize organization information systems. Therefore, the extra effort of the working group is the determinant factor of making computerization feasible in the social welfare agency. Various development stages of FOS's computerization showed that the computerization should start at structured tasks. Finally, according to the implementation strategies of FOS's computerization, it has provided sufficient training to users, involved professionals in the development of the information systems and provided easy access to technological support. It also has paid attention to the structural factors of the organization that could impede the adoption of computer technology. It should be highlighted that the case presented above is still tentative and needs to be studied in more detail.

Reflection on MIS Computerization

The adoption of new technology and its effects on an organization is a complex and important topic for social welfare administrators. A better understanding of the combined effectiveness of technical, organizational, and user-related issues can substantially help administrators, practitioners and developers of computerization in obtaining knowledge on the adoption and the effects of the use of the computer in establishing the management information system.

Total Involvement in Computerization

Computerization is not simply a process of shifting from manual work to computer operation. It brings changes to the whole organization. The practice of data collection in the frontline would be changed to adapt to the requirement of the computer format. The feasibility of direct access to raw data by supervisors would also change the monitoring, control and coordination functions. With the help of computers in processing bulky data, top management can have more information support in decision making and strategies formulation. Since the changes may exist in the organization throughout the computerization process, the total involvement of staff is unavoidable, whether or not they are involved actively or passively.

On the other hand, it must be highlighted that the success of computerization is highly affected by the support of the management. As the changes may exist in the organization by installing computers, many new managerial issues such as re-deployment of manpower, re-structuring of information flow and resistance from staff, etc. must be handled. Furthermore, the computerization does not involve merely the installation of additional hardware and software, but also a long term investment on the system maintenance, staff training and technology advancement. If the proposal is initiated or supported by the management of an organization, the chance of success will be higher. Since working groups or committees are responsible for devising a master plan and monitoring its realization, appropriate representation of top management is essential for the effectiveness of the working group or the committee.

In short, different levels and functional departments of the organization would have different information needs. Their involvement in the computerization process may safeguard the usefulness of the information systems for its users. Empirically, a local study on the use of computer in children and youth centres reflected that the user participation in the computerization process was the significant factor to enhance computer use (Au, 1995).

Technological Support

Lack of knowledge in computer and computerization is so far the main restraint of the introduction of new information technology in social welfare agencies, as long as they are not subsidized to develop computerized information systems. Human service professionals may not have rich knowledge on information technology to facilitate the agency's computerization. In addition, computer proficiency seems to be an extra requirement for the human service professionals to perform their direct service functions. In fact, the development of computer technology is far beyond the understanding of social welfare professionals. Therefore, we do not need to pursue the new generation of computer technology. We need a new generation of social welfare staff who can use the computer with care, creativity and patience in order to enhance their service quality. A generation of social welfare staff with computer experience requires well-planned training and education. Social welfare administrators should also create a favourable working environment and provide the necessary condition for their centre staff to draw upon the power of computers.

On the contrary, if there are some computer elites in an agency, management would suspect that the introduction of computerized information systems might lead to a loss of their power due to a continuing dependence on these computer expertise on information processing. In fact, the primary duty of these social welfare staff is direct frontline service rather than the operation of computers. To solve this dilemma, the top management, apart from getting involved in the development of computerization, should also employ some computer technologists in order to have a smooth computerization process and maintenance.

Resistance to Change

Imagine you are being employed in a social welfare agency for many years and suddenly there are some young colleagues and your supervisor propose the installation of computers in the agency. Naturally you may resist it because the computerization induces a great change on your working pattern and the centralization of service and clientele information which determines the value of appraisal on your performance.

In fact, the introduction of new systems annoys staff for the following reasons:

1. It replaces current functions and, hence, causes the elimination of work control of some staff.
2. It stimulates changes in organizational structures and, hence, in power and authority.

3. It modifies current operation procedures and, hence, generate confusion and uncertainty.
4. It requires the establishment of more structured activities and, hence, reduces the prestige of the "old stars" of the manual systems. Moreover, while disclosing current operation procedures, it may bring discredit to employees whose practices are not always strictly regulated.

Resistance to change reflects that either the staff are not motivated enough or they fear changes more than they value probable benefits. There are also several arguments that can soften resistance to change. In the case of FOS, the following reasons have successfully convinced reluctant staff of the need for changes.

1. The current state is really bad and may lead to re-staffing after the Centre Review, so that jobs are not as secure as they seem to be. Therefore, something must be done to enhance the service effectiveness and accountability to the government.
2. A computerized system will release clerks from repeated routine tasks and leave them to share the clerical tasks of program staff. In return, the productivity of professionals can be magnified.
3. Acquiring experience of handling a computerized system is very important nowadays and thus expands job opportunities and prospects for the operation staff.
4. Computerized systems increase the capacity for future growth. Agency performance will be improved and so will its prestige.

In addition to these persuasions, intense user involvement during system design, together with appropriate education and training, will probably assist in change management.

Training of Staff

We can easily design and program an excellent information system, but if we do not plan its implementation well, we might ruin the entire project. As an organization gets in the process of computerization, the transformation and implementation stages are the crux of the whole process. These stages deal with the actual installation of the newly produced computerized information system in the organization. This involves various issues such as training, testing, file transformation and procedure changes. Each of the issues requires delicate and careful treatment. Most of them involve users of various ranks who might not be familiar with computer technology, and therefore could be sensitive and even hostile towards the change. However, negative reaction can be weakened or suspended if the staff involved understand the purpose and benefits of the system and also know how to operate it. Computers become more friendly to staff when they are no longer mysterious. Therefore training is the most important part of implementing the information systems. Training may have two goals: (1) providing a general understanding of the system and (2) acquiring technical skills to run it. The Au's (1995) study affirmed this argument that user training, especially informal training, is a significant factor affecting the computer use in children and youth centres.

In the case of FOS, CICs have to be familiar with operational techniques to an extent that they are able to supervise their centre staff to run the relevant systems. Furthermore, CICs are also required to have a profound understanding of the ideological background that the information systems will contribute to their better performance. Otherwise, they will be reluctant to enforce its use. On the other hand, operational staff — usually the clerical assistants in centre service — should also have some ideological background, which can better motivate them to accept the system, but for them greater emphasis should be placed on practical issues. In short, if we overload CICs with technical details, or if we burden the clerical assistants with too much ideology, we might lose our audience and ruin the whole training plan. An appropriate mix of both should be carefully blended in a well-planned training program.

Transformation from Manual to Computerized System

Every new computerized information system replaces something that was prevailed before, may it be an old computerized system or a set of manual procedures. The transition from the old to the new system is extremely delicate because there is hidden conflicts or interests between the implementers and the rest of the organization. Sometimes, the implementers would like to have some sort of breaks to spare more time to prepare the system for use. However, the organization may not be able to afford a break. The system must maintain the continuity of its operations because the organization handles many activities, of which the information system is only a small segment. Since the implementers must comply with the organization interests, they have to plan the transformation so that continuity can be preserved and interruption of normal activities be minimal.

In the case of FOS, the transformation from manual to computerized system took a whole year in order to safeguard the continuity of the center services. There was also a period of time in the beginning stage of computerization that the manual and the computer operation proceeded at the same time. Such an arrangement could secure the preservation of information in the process of transition. The operational staff of various centres has been overloaded for a year. It is termed the parallel approach. Both the old and new systems run in parallel for one year to ensure a smooth system transformation. At the beginning of the period the old system would be the major one while the new would only be a trial in order to verify its reliability. At the latter part of the parallel period, the new system would become the major one, but the old one would still be maintained for backup and control. Only after the new system performs satisfactorily could the old one be refused. This approach is very safe, but it is also very expensive because operating costs are nearly doubled during the transitional period.

Conclusion

This paper is actually a case report about establishing a MIS through computers. With the insights from the literature review of MIS and the case illustration of FOS's computerization, experience can be consolidated in a more systematic way. The key issues of the computerization in FOS which are discussed above, though neither comprehensive nor exhaustive, can be a reference for other social welfare agencies which want to develop their MIS with computers in the future.

References

Ahituv, N. and Neumann, S. (1990) *Principles of Information System for Management*, 3rd Ed. WM.C. Brown Publishers, USA.

Amoako-Gyampah, K. and White, K.B. (1993) User involvement and user satisfaction, *Information & Management*, **25**, 1–10.

Au, W.C. (1995) *User Factors and Computer Use of Children and Youth Centres in Hong Kong*. MA Dissertation, The Hong Kong Polytechnic University.

Benbenishty, R. (1989) Designing Computerized Clinical Information System to Monitor Interventions on the Agency Level, *Computer in Human Services*, **5**(1/2), 69–88.

Boyd, L.H., Jr., Hylton, J.H., and Price, S.V. (1978) Computers in social work practice: A review, *Social Work*, September, 268–371.

Chan, K.T. & et al. (1992) *Variables Affecting the Pattern of Activities of First-Line Administrators in Voluntary Welfare Sectors in Hong Kong*. Hong Kong Polytechnic.

Cooper, C.R. (1989) The integration of computerized application in child welfare oversight agency, *Computer in Human Services,* **4**(1/2), 141–152.

Cuvo, D., Hall, F., and Mailder, G.R. (1988) Computerizing central intake: A means toward accountability, *Social Case: The Journal of Contemporary Social Work*, April, 214–224.

Davis, G.B. & Olson, M.H. (1984) *Management Information Systems-conceptual foundations, structure and development*, 2nd Ed. McGraw-Hill Book Company, Singapore.

Finnegan, D.J. & Ivanoff, A. (Winter 1991) Effects of brief computer training on attitudes toward computer use in practice: An educational experiment, *Journal of Social Work Education*, **27**(1), 73–82.

Garcia, R.R., (1988) *Human Factors in Systems Development*. NCC Publications, England.

Gorry, G.A., & Merton, M.S.S. (Fall 1971) A Framework for management information system, *Sloan Management Review*.

Grasso, A.J. & Epstein, I. (1989) The Boysville experience: Integrating practice decision-making, program evaluation, and management information, *Computers in Human Services*, **4**(1/2), 85–94.

Hirschheim, R.A., (1989) User participation in practice: Experiences with participative systems design. In Knight, K., (ed.), Unicom Seminars Limited, London. *Participation in Systems Development*, Chapter Twelve, pp. 194–204.

HKCSS, Children and Youth Division, *The Minutes of the 3rd Meeting of the Coordinating Committee on Children and Youth Centre (1994–95)*.

HKCSS, *Welfare Digest*, **93**(233), 4–6.

Hoshino, G. and McDonald, T.P. (1975) Agencies in the computer age, *Social Work*, January, 10–14.

Knight, K., (ed) (1989) *Participation in Systems Development*, Introduction, pp. 1–8. Unicom Seminars Limited, London.

Law, C.K. (1986) *A Job Task Analysis on the Social Welfare Personnel in Youth Centres*. MBA Dissertation, Chinese University of Hong Kong.

Lodge, L.J. (1989) A user-led model of systems development. In Knight, K. (ed.), *Participation in Systems Development*, Chapter Two, pp. 34–59. Unicom Seminars Limited, London.

Mak, D. and Lee, M.K. (1984) *Task Analysis of Front-line Social Workers in Hong Kong*, Hong Kong Polytechnic.

Mumford, E., (1989) User participation in a changing environment: Why we need it. In Knight, K. (ed.), *Participation in Systems Development*, Chapter Three, pp. 60–72. Unicom Seminars Limited, London.

Murphy, J.W. *et al.* (Summer 1987) Conceptual issues related to the use of computers in social work practice, *Journal of Independent Social Work*, **1**(4), 63–73.

Mutschler, E. and Cnaan, R.A. (Spring 1985) Success and failure of computerized information systems: Two case studies in human service agencies, *Administration in Social Work,* **9**(1), 67–79.

Mutschler, E. and Hoefer, R. (1990) Factors affecting the use of computer technology in human service organization, *Administration in Social Work*, **14**, 87–101.

Newhart, D.M.N. (1991) *An analysis of the effects of computer usage and computer trining on white-collar performance evaluation in the insurance industry.* Ph.D. Dissertation, U.M.I.

Nurius, P.S., Hooyman, N. and Nicoll, A.E. (1991) Computers in agencies: A survey baseline and planning implications, *Journal of Social Service Research*, **14**(3/4), 141–155.

Olson, M. and Ives, B. (1981) User involvement in systems design: An empirical test of alternative approaches, *Information & Management*, **4**.

Schoech, D. (1990) *Human Service Computing-concepts & Applications*. Haworth Press, Inc. N.Y.

______, (1982) *Computer Use in Human Services: A Guide To Information Management*. Human Sciences Press, Inc. N.Y.

______, (1979) A microcomputer based human service information system, *Administration in Social Work*, **3**(4), Winter, 423–439.

Slavin, S. (ed) (1978) *Social Administration: The Management of The Social Services*. The Haworth Press, New York.

Sullivan, R.J. (1980) Human issues in computerized social services, *Child Welfare*, **LIX**(7) July/August, 401–407.

Tricker, R.I. (1993), *Harnessing Information Power*. Hong Kong University Press, Hong Kong.

Working Party on the Review of Children and Youth Centres Services (1984) *Report of the Review of Children and Youth Centres Services*, Hong Kong Government.

10

Designing Performance Indicators for an Experimental Project: Multi-disciplinary Team for Elderly Street Sleepers

LAM Wan Cheung, Winnie

Introduction

Social service evaluation is seldom an easy job. Evaluation on the performance of an experimental service, where comparable performance standards could not be easily identified, is all the more difficult. However, being the major financial controller and thus monitoring body of social welfare services in Hong Kong, the Social Welfare Department has to commit itself to such a task. The implementation of an experimental project named Multi-disciplinary Team for Elderly Street Sleepers (MDTESS) was due for evaluation in November 1999. It is necessary to look into the worthiness of both the continuous financial support to the service and to the Team in particular. Development of performance indicators to facilitate the evaluation is thus needed.

In the design process, literature review of theoretical concepts as well as of the Team, integration of theory into the practical situations, putting ideas into practice, review of and reflections about the practice which will then lead to revision of implementation of the theory, etc. form a natural cycle of the action plan. This allows continuous refinement and improvement in the design. While the present exercise of designing performance indicators is more of a design plan than having the indicators put into practice for service evaluation for the MDTESS for the time being, review and reflections are more at a theoretical level but are not necessarily restrictive. Finally, the report aims at providing a documentary record of the above process.

In the first part of the report, we would look into the background the MDTESS which provides an organizational context for which the design process takes place. Some literature review of the concept of performance indicators would be recorded, which includes also the types of performance indicators, the process of designing performance indicators, and some suggested considerations throughout the process. The concepts above will then be put into practice for the design of performance indicators for the MDTESS. Specific characteristics and evaluation criteria for MDTESS are taken into consideration, and a set of performance indicators is then proposed. Throughout this action plan of designing performance indicators, certain concern and reflections are addressed, which are shared in the final part of this report.

Background of the MDTESS

In November 1993, a Working Group on Care for the Elderly (WGCE) was appointed to review the services for the elderly and to identify directions for future development. In the Working Group's Report published in August 1994, it was mentioned that "elderly street sleepers are a disadvantaged and vulnerable group which requires help. The problems of elderly street sleepers are usually multi-faceted. They need special assistance to help resolve their problems". It is also recommended that "a multi-disciplinary team should be established to provide intensive outreach service to street sleepers, with special emphasis given to homeless elderly persons", and that "the project should be funded by the Lotteries Fund on an experimental basis" (WGCE, 1994, p. v).

It was against such a background that the Multi-disciplinary Team for Elderly Street Sleepers was set up. A non-government organization (NGO) had been selected to run the experimental service to serve the elderly street sleepers in the West Kowloon Region where the highest number of elderly street sleepers were found. The service came into operation in June 1996 and would be due for evaluation in November 1999 for consideration on the worthiness of the service and continuous financial support for the project.

The MDTESS aimed at providing an intensive outreach service to street sleepers, with special emphasis to help rehouse elderly persons and reintegrate them into the society. With a view to achieve this goal, five objectives were then stated:

(1) To help rehouse homeless elderly street sleepers;
(2) To help elderly street sleepers improve their personal hygiene even if they choose to remain on the streets;
(3) To establish and maintain elderly street sleepers' communication with helping professionals;
(4) To strengthen elderly street sleepers' understanding of community resources, e.g. temporary accommodation facilities, compassionate rehousing, elderly homes, rehabilitation institutions, day relief centres for street sleepers, counselling service, social security assistance, etc.;
(5) To enhance elderly street sleepers' motivation for receiving assistance.

With regard to the above objectives, MDTESS was expected to perform the following tasks:

(1) To establish a friendly relationship with elderly street sleepers;
(2) To provide counselling and escort service to the elderly street sleepers for medical treatment, applications for various assistance, etc.;
(3) To persuade them to live away from the streets by assisting them to secure a temporary or permanent accommodation;
(4) To provide nursing care and health care advice, particularly to those who are drug addicts, mentally ill or alcoholic;
(5) To design and implement health care programmes for them;
(6) To recruit and train volunteers in paying concern visits to elderly street sleepers.

The MDTESS was comprised of three team members to perform the above tasks, namely a team leader at the Assistant Social Work Officer rank, a welfare worker at the Welfare Worker rank, and a nurse at the Registered Nurse rank. The team leader had to supervise the team and take the lead in rendering outreaching service; the welfare worker had to assist the team leader in rendering services and running programmes; while the nurse, apart from joining the team in outreaching duties, rendered nursing and health care services and implemented health care programmes. (For details of team organization and duties, please refer to Appendix 1.)

Concepts on Performance Indicators

Perspectives in Performance Measurement

Sets of performance indicators are designed for measurement of the performance of a particular unit/service. Performance measurement traditionally refers to the evaluation on the aspects of economy, efficiency and effectiveness. Economy "is concerned with minimizing the cost of resources acquired or used, having regard to the quality of the inputs"; efficiency refers to "the relationship between the output of goods, services or others results and the resources used to produce them" and "how far is maximum output achieved for a given input or minimum input used for a given output"; while effectiveness concerns "the relationship between the intended results and the actual results of projects, programmes, or other activities" and "how successfully do outputs of goods, services or other results achieve policy objectives, operational goals and other intended effects" (Jackson & Palmer, 1989, p. 50).

However, scholars have added to these aspects some other elements and perspectives. Among them, equity and quality are worth mentioning. Equity implies that "in all similar cases individuals will be dealt with alike" and refers to "neutrality and fairness between different groups" (Carter, Klein & Day, 1992, pp. 39–40). Quality is concerned with "whether the process of providing goods or services is running smoothly and is tuned to consumer requirements" (Carter, Klein & Day, 1992, p. 174).

Organizational Characteristics

Carter, Klein and Day also stressed the importance of understanding organizational characteristics in designing performance indicators. Various paradigms have been discussed and some of them are quite relevant to our considerations for evaluation of the MDTESS, including heterogeneity, complexity and the uncertainty level of the service. Heterogeneity means "the number of different products or services provided" with the assumption that "assessing the performance of a single-product organization is less difficult than assessing that of a multi-product organization"; complexity refers to "the extent to which an organization has to mobilize a number of different skills in order to deliver its services or produce its goods"; while uncertainty concerns "the causal relationship between input of resources and the achievement of stated objectives" (Carter, Klein & Day, 1992, p. 32).

Dimensional Considerations

Apart from organizational characteristics, what affects our emphasis in designing performance indicators includes also the purpose of performance measurement and thus the dimensions of performance indicators (classified into structural, process and outcome measures). In case the performance measurement aims at making individual appraisals, greater emphasis might be placed on areas of process and outcome dimensions. On the other hand, if it aims at improving day-to-day management, emphasis might also be given to the structural dimension as well.

As the MDTESS is to be evaluated on various aspects for consideration of continuous financial support, all three dimensions might be included in the evaluation exercise, though each might carry a different weight. Further discussion on this would be made in the latter part of the report.

Types of Performance Indicators

In designing performance indicators, it is essential to take note that there are three types of classification, namely, prescriptive, descriptive and proscriptive indicators. Prescriptive indicators are "linked to particular objectives" (Jackson & Palmer, 1989, p. 51) and are "used to monitor progress towards their achievement". They have the advantage of being "measurable" (Carter, Klein & Day, 1992, p. 49). Descriptive indicators are "a multitude of statistics which describe what a department does, in other words, its activities and throughputs" (Jackson & Palmer, 1989, p. 51), and they emphasize "travelling along a particular route" or "in a particular direction" (Carter, Klein & Day, 1992, p. 50). Finally, proscriptive indicators are "negative indicator" (Jackson & Palmer, 1989, p. 51) which operates "like an alarm-bell", "giving warning that things are happening which should not be tolerated in a well-run organization" (Carter, Klein & Day, 1992, p. 50).

Prescriptive indicators might give a clearer target and more quantifiable measurement than descriptive indicators, but the choice of which indicators to go by depends on the situational requirements and feasibility.

Basis of Comparison

Finally, indicators are set to evaluate whether the performance of the organization or service is good or bad. Thus, standard-setting is required for the purpose of comparison. Carter, Klein and Day suggest four types of comparisons, namely, targets, time-series, comparable organizational units and external comparison. Targets comparison simply refers to the "analysis of performance against the achievement of targets"; time-series is the "comparison with the historical record of the same organization"; comparable organizational units uses "a cross-sectional comparison with other units of the same service"; while external comparison is to "look at the performance of other organizations" which is seldom widely used since measurement for one type of service or organization might not be transferable for another type (Carter, Klein & Day, 1992, p. 46–48).

Staff Involvement

Finally, in the process of the design and implementation of performance measurement, the importance of staff involvement has always been emphasized. Performance indicators should be meaningful to the staff, and "only if they feel ownership of the measures" would they "feel motivated to make effective use of performance measure" and "this implies that they have a say in what types of measure will be used" (Jackson & Palmer, 1989, p. 25).

Designing Process

The main steps involved in designing performance indicators, as suggested by Jackson and Palmer, are:
(1) Deciding on what is to be measured, which requires the activities of analyzing the objectives of the organization/service, which, in this case, is the MDTESS;
(2) Deciding on which measures are to be used, that is selecting the performance indicators to match the objectives;
(3) While designing the indicators, a valid basis of comparison or yardstick should also be selected;
(4) Sources of data should be ascertained;
(5) Designing supportive data collection systems, that is the data collection method; and
(6) Determining the presentation method.

We would then proceed to the design of performance indicators for the evaluation of the MDTESS, using Jackson and Palmer's model as a reference for the procedural steps, while taking into consideration the above mentioned perspectives, characteristics and dimensional concerns.

Designing Performance Indicators for the MDTESS

Characteristics of the MDTESS

Before going into the design process, certain characteristics of the MDTESS have to be taken into considerations, particularly regarding its heterogeneity, complexity and uncertainty.

Firstly, corresponding to the particular concern over the problem of elderly street sleepers thus the background of the setting up of MDTESS, its target clientele has been confined to:

(1) elderly street sleepers who are not known cases to the Social Welfare Department or any welfare agencies;
(2) known elderly street sleepers cases who require nursing care or preliminary health assessment; and
(3) suspected elderly street sleepers.

With regard to these clientele, their problems are often multi-faceted and the most common major problems are:

(1)   Health problems including suspected mental illness, suspected senile dementia, physical disability/illness, very poor personal hygiene, etc.
(2)   Social problems including relationship problem, drug addiction, alcoholism, financial problem, etc.

Considering the above, both heterogeneity and complexity of the MDTES are high in the sense that the multi-faceted problems of the elderly street sleepers require intensive service and diverse skills in assisting them, and the expected service outcome could hardly be simply rehousing them. Besides, simple relations between the MDTESS' outputs with the final aim of rehousing them is doubtful as street sleepers' problems could be affected by various elements. High degree of uncertainty on this causal relationship is also observed.

We would go into further details on how these characteristics affect our design of performance indicators in the following part of analyzing the objectives of the MDTESS, that is what is to be measured.

Analyzing the Objectives of MDTESS

With the various stated aims, objectives and tasks of the MDTESS, we need to understand which are the core values of the project, that is what are the most critical elements that we want to measure.

Despite the final aim of the MDTESS to rehouse the elderly street sleepers, this could hardly be the only intended outcome of the project. The MDTESS is specifically designed to deal with elderly street sleepers and those with nursing and health care needs. These are probably the hard core cases which require a long-term intensive service and a proactive approach before they could be motivated to accept the assistance offered by the MDTESS. In fact, they might be initially helped to hold a more accepting attitude towards the helping professionals before they could be encouraged to explore more about the resources available to them and to have greater motivation to receive those services. These are probably the "process-objectives" before the final one of rehousing them be actualized.

This relationship between the objectives is illustrated in the flow chart in Figure 1. Besides, considering the complex and uncertain nature of the service, the service outputs could hardly be directly linked to the final

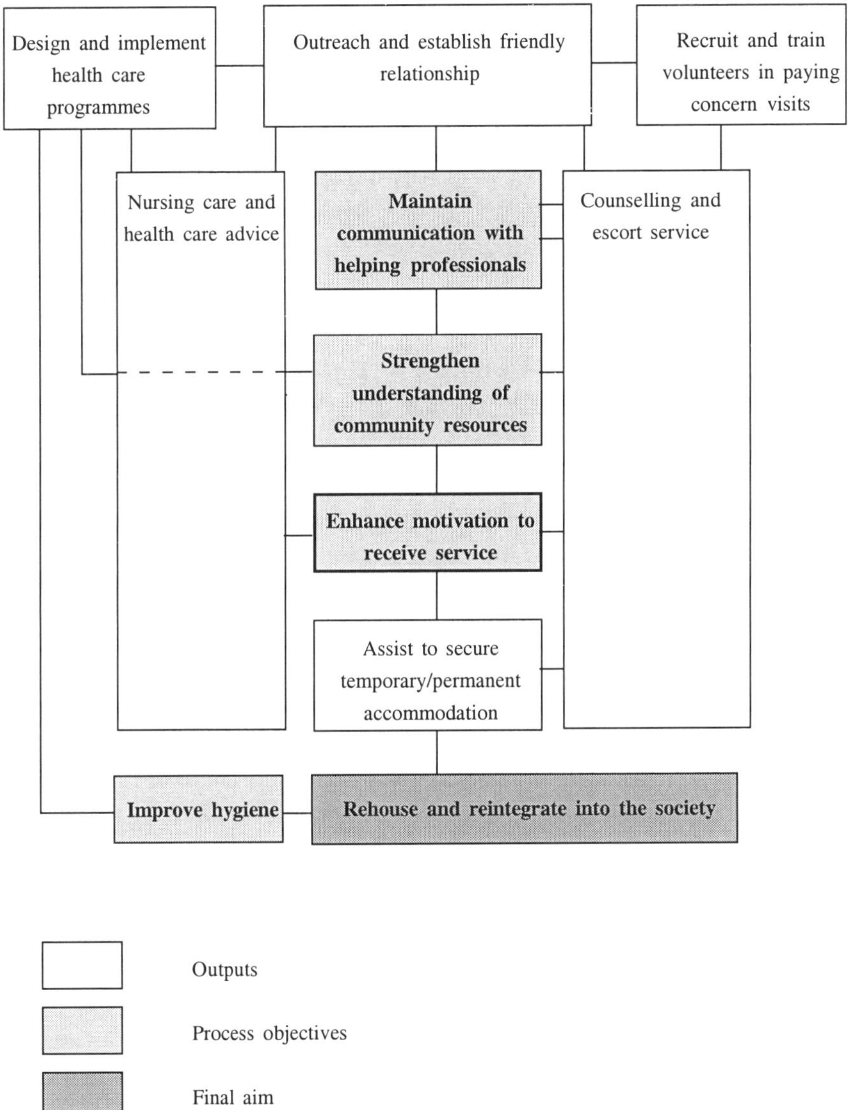

Fig. 1: Relationship between the outputs and the expected outcomes/objectives.

outcome but the relationship between outputs and the "process objectives" instead seems more realistic. Therefore, instead of evaluating the service effectiveness simply on the achievement of the final aim of rehousing these clients, the "process objectives" should gain more emphasis.

Apart from the measurement of the effectiveness of the MDTESS which is surely vital for the consideration of the continuous survival of the service, efficiency is another basic aspect for considering continuous support to the project. The assessment of outputs in relation to inputs is a common requirement for the evaluation of social services. With the stated input of manpower, an expected quantity of outputs which should be comparable to other similar service units should be achieved. Besides, with the target clientele specified, the MDTESS is expected to concentrate its efforts on serving the specified group so that the service could achieve greater efficiency in helping the clients.

As the service is expected to take a proactive approach by rendering intensive outreaching service so that the often "non-reachable elderly street sleepers" could be contacted and moved, it is worthwhile to access the equity of the service. However, as mentioned, the clients are often "non-reachable" and rarely would they approach the MDTESS for service, nor are they willing to receive service. Measuring their applications to the MDTESS for service would surely be unrealistic. Instead, the sources of referrals might give an easier and more feasible indication.

The traditional performance measurement evaluates also the economy perspective. For the MDTESS, it could be expected that it would not be a cheap service in terms of the money input and the expected outcome on the number of elderly street sleepers rehoused, even as these cases, being hard core, require a long term service. It might not be fair to compare this service with other street sleepers services where the target clientele might not be completely the same. Nevertheless, the cost aspect is also worth evaluating to facilitate cost estimation of the service in the future.

Finally, there is also the quality perspective. With the basic intention to help elderly street sleepers, whether the outputs of the staff are relevant to the benefits of clients or they are doing what the latter consider as quality service is an important element in assessing the performance of the project. Besides, with the increasing emphasis on the quality of social services, this aspect definitely should not be disregarded. Domains of service quality concerning the quality outputs rendered to the clients, management quality with regard to the operation and management of the service unit, as well as staff quality would be assessed.

Proposing Performance Indicators for the MDTESS

Having identified the essential evaluation domains and the critical standards/criteria, we now proceed to the design of indicators for each domain and standard. While we can refer to the table on Appendix 2 on the proposed performance indicators with the sources of data and ways of collection, the rationale on choices of measures is hereby discussed.

Regarding the measurement on effectiveness of the project, outcome indicators would surely be adopted. The achievement of the final aim of rehousing elderly street sleepers would of course be measured, which could be done simply by a numeric count on the numbers of elderly street sleepers rehoused. However, as mentioned in previous parts, the "process objectives" including the client's willingness in maintaining communication with the helping professionals and the achievement of helping the clients to have more understanding on the community resources, enhancing their motivation to receive services and improving their hygiene should be emphasized. Instead of merely quantifiable statistical information, the attitude and degree of hygiene of the clients, and their understanding of and motivation for receiving community resources are to be measured. The numbers of clients whose living standard improve or deteriorate can serve as an indicator. Obviously, to reveal the service effectiveness, the numbers making progress should outweigh the numbers experiencing deterioration. In fact, this not only helps to measure the service effectiveness, but also helps the MDTESS monitor the progress of its clients.

For other domains and perspectives, mixtures of dimensions of indicators might be used. For the efficiency perspective, both the process indicators, that is the activities outputs and structural indicators (profile on the cases and caseload) have been adopted. Activities outputs include the number of visits conducted and the number of groups and programmes organized. Profile on the cases refers to the size of the target clientele (elderly street sleepers and those requiring nursing and health care service), and this shows whether efforts have been made to the intended client group for efficient delivery of service. Profile on the caseload refers to the number of active, potential and new contact cases, the cases turnover rate and the duration of the closed cases. This again helps to show the distribution of the team's effort and their efficiency in helping the cases.

While the economy and equity perspectives require only a few structural indicators — the actual cost per case against the estimated cost and the profile on sources of referral (the number of referral from each source) respectively — the measurement of the quality domain is difficult. A mix of structural, process and outcome indicators is required. Regarding the service quality, process indicators with regard to the types and numbers of groups/programmes/concern visits/escorts should be assessed to see whether appropriate services have been delivered to satisfy clients' respective needs and solve their problems. Furthermore, to show whether these outputs are meeting the client's expectations or welcomed by them, attendance of these activities, which is in fact an outcome indicator of the activities, is also included. Finally, as rendering proactive outreaching service is one of the specific characteristics of the MDTESS, the quality of outreaching service should also be assessed. In this regard, the structural aspects of the time schedule of outreaching sessions per week are checked to see whether the team is scheduling for the elderly street sleepers' sake.

As for management quality and staff quality, mainly process indicators of numbers of staff meetings and supervision, and whether compliance on the documentation and account requirement has been observed, and structural indicators on the profile of the qualified staff would be adopted respectively.

Basis of Comparison

To decide whether the MDTESS is performing well or badly by the indicators, a basis of comparison should be identified for references. At present, we compare the service unit to be evaluated with service norms which is derived from comparable service units.

With regard to the evaluation of the MDTESS, it is not easy to identify comparable service units in view of its experimental nature. Reviewing the existing services for street sleepers, day relief centres (DRCs) for street sleepers offers probably the most similar service type. It is possible to compare the MDTESS with DRCs in outputs measures (caseload, case/programme activities per worker) and some of the quality outputs (types and number of groups/programmes, number of compliments and complaints, etc., but not those concerning outreaching activities and nursing/health care services). Besides, it would be unfair to compare the outcome measures because of the differences in the clientele between the two services: street sleepers who attend DRC would probably be relatively younger and more independent while MDTESS' cases are mostly old, with ill-health and are more socially withdrawn.

In fact, for MDTESS, other comparison measures are also employed. Targets have been used for the clientele as the team is expected to serve the specified clientele of elderly street sleepers. Besides, targets of compliance with documentation and financial account procedures, and of the number of qualified staff are set. On the other hand, time-series is used as a basis of comparison. Despite the project's being experimental and short in time bind, we would try to compare the client's level of such attitude and functioning from case opening to case closure by measuring the outcome achievement of clients' improvement in personal hygiene, relationship with the helping professionals, and understanding of and motivation for receiving community resources.

Identification of the basis of comparison has been the most difficult task in the design of performance measurement for the MDTESS. Being an experimental project, there is no historical record of the same or similar service, nor could we set targets for it except for some nominal outputs activities. In other words, application of prescriptive indicators is not easy in this evaluation exercise. Besides, it is expected that this project could throw light on the support-worthiness and future development of the service. Therefore, a combination of descriptive, prescriptive and proscriptive indicators is employed.

Sources and Method of Data Collection, and Presentation of Data

Any burdensome record and reporting should be avoided so that the MDTESS could concentrate on their effort in rendering intensive outreaching services to help elderly street sleepers. However, being an experimental project, there are various aspects that should be evaluated, which require the production of relevant information and documents. Therefore, in considering sources the of data for performance measurement, we have to strike a balance between gathering sufficient information for evaluation purpose and not affecting the team's service delivery. Thus, collection of data from existing records should be adopted. For information on the outputs measures, it would be best collected from the statistical record, which the team completes monthly just as any other street sleepers services do. Whereas, for some other non-numerical indicators, agency records and financial records (for those on cost measurement) could be utilized. However, considering the outcome measure, although it would be possible to count the numbers of street sleepers being rehoused using the statistical record, it would be difficult to count on the achievement of "process objectives" including the improvement in hygiene, understanding of community resources, and motivation to receive services, etc. Thus, a number of case assessment forms have been designed since the implementation of the project to help the MDTESS make records on the progress of each case. (A Sample of the statistical form and case assessment forms are available on Appendices 4 and 5.) The implementation of the case assessment forms is so designed that, while it facilitates the evaluation of the achievement of the MDTESS, it helps the team monitor its work progress with the clients.

For details regarding the data collection for each performance indicator, please refer to the table on the proposed performance indicators for the MDTESS on Appendix 3.

Finally, with the various data collected, it is necessary to translate it into easily comprehensible information. Tables and charts would be useful tools for a presentation of the data. For simple comparison like the actual cost against the estimated cost, some bar charts might be applicable. When percentages among the total like the number of elderly street sleepers among total caseload, are to be presented, pie charts might be a good choice. Besides, in order to show any progress on the achievements (in terms of both outputs and outcomes) of the MDTESS, linear charts on which the statistics at different time points are plotted could be employed. The above are simply suggestions on the possible presentation methods, while more of other methods should not be neglected.

Staff Involvement

As discussed in the early parts of this report, staff involvement in the process of performance measurement is necessary. This is of course also applicable to the evaluation of the MDTESS. Nevertheless, the degree of staff participation of the staff, in this case, the NGO, is worth stating. The objectives of the MDTESS have been set but the evaluation criteria are discussed with the NGO, both the project's team staff and the administrative staff. They are involved in the consideration of what the core values of the project are and the critical aspects to be measured. It is thus agreed that instead of measuring only the final aim of rehousing the elderly street sleepers, the "process objectives" should be of great emphasis to this experimental project. Besides, evaluation through the set performance indicators in fact helps the team to monitor the progress of their work, which is helpful in their consideration for any revision of their intervention strategies. Therefore, the involvement of the NGO staff in the process helps them recognize the importance of this evaluation as well as become aware of the possible activities required in conducting such an evaluation. In other words, they are more well prepared in the collection and reporting of the data required, which would surely facilitate the evaluation process.

Conclusion and Reflections

The formulation of design of performance indicators, through literature review on the subject, provides the foundation of understanding into the role of performance measurement in service evaluation as well as various evaluation perspectives of economy, efficiency and effectiveness, and also equity, quality, etc. as some scholars added. Concerns for organizational characteristics such as heterogeneity, complexity and uncertainty of the service and the purpose of evaluation and thus the dimensions of measurement are addressed. On the other hand, the stated design process also provides a framework for my exercise of designing performance indicators for the experimental project MDTESS to base on.

Nevertheless, throughout the present design process, which aims to make integration of theoretical concepts into practice for the evaluation of the MDTESS, the characteristics of the service or service unit to be evaluated plays an important role in affecting the employment of various considerations and techniques. With the specified clientele of the MDTESS of elderly street sleepers (most of them having stayed in the streets for years and are hard core cases with multi-faceted problems) and those with nursing and health care needs (very often with suspected mental problems), to expect direct feedback from these clients in terms of service effectiveness and quality is in fact very difficult. The characteristics of the clientele also affects our consideration on which are the feasible or reachable objectives and thus ultimately affects the emphasis on the evaluation of outcome achievement.

Besides, the purpose of evaluation being the evaluation of support-worthiness of the service also affects the focus of evaluation; service effectiveness might gain more attention. (This could be understood as when the purpose is for service improvement, more attention might be given to the efficiency and quality perspectives, and the dimensions of measurement would also be revised accordingly.)

Finally, being an experimental service, it is a very difficult task to identify other service units that are really comparable and when the setting of targets is fairly without direction. This leads to the employment of more descriptive indicators with the combination of prescriptive and proscriptive ones. Nevertheless, as one of the purposes of experimental projects is to reveal the service needs or clients' expectations, that is the market of the specific service, and to give directions on the future development of the service, such a combination ratio would be acceptable. Besides, if the service is proved to be effective and receives subvention in the future, it would surely be required to enter into Funding and Services Agreement and be subject to the requirements of the Service Quality Standards. By then, agreed outputs/quality outputs would be expected and the performance indicators might probably be revised to be more prescriptive than descriptive.

As a final conclusion, this exercise reflects the need for a flexible adoption of theoretical approaches and methods in the design of performance indicators, considering the organizational and service characteristics and actual situation. In other words, a contingent approach on top of the basic theoretical foundation is never a failing requirement.

Besides, the design process is seldom a closed end process. Continuous review on the feasibility and practicality of the employment of the set performance indicators, and revision of the indicators should always be taken into consideration.

References

Attkisson, C. Clifford, Hargreaves, William A., Horowitz, Mardi J. & Sorensen, James E. (1978) *Evaluation of Human Service Programs*. USA, Academic Press.

Blythe, Betty J. & Tripodi, Tony (1989) *Measurement in Direct Practice*. USA, Sage Publications.

Carter, Neil, Klein, Rudolf & Day, Patricia (1992) *How Organizations Measure Success: The Use of Performance Indicators in Government*. UK, Routledge.

Cheetham, Juliet, Fuller, Roger, McIvor, Gill & Petch, Alison (1992) *Evaluating Social Work Effectiveness*. UK, Open University Press.

Jackson, Peter & Palmer, Bob (1989) *First Steps in Measuring Performance in the Public Sector: A Management Guide*. UK, Public Finance Foundation.

Appendix 1

Staff Provision of MDTESS

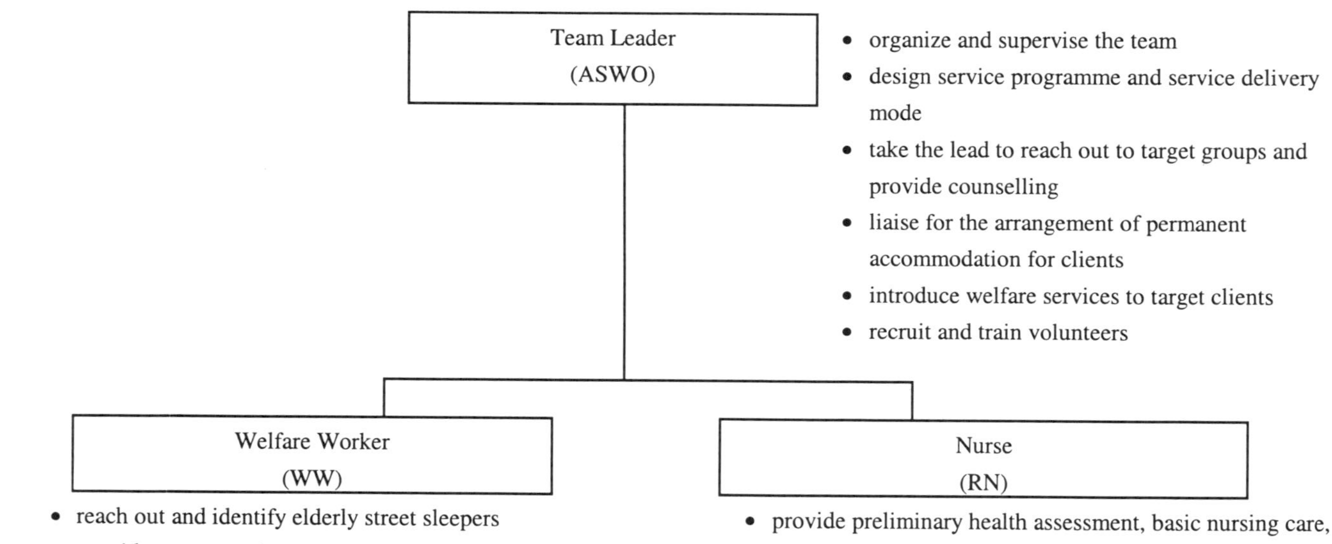

Appendix 2

Proposed Performance Indicators for MDTESS

Standard / Criteria	Indicators	Calculation / Formula	Source of Data	Frequency of Data Collection
Economy Perspective				
1. *Cost*	i. Actual cost against estimated cost per case	$ / case %	Financial account record	End of experimental period
Efficiency Perspective				
1. *Clientele*	i. No. of elderly street sleepers served among total caseload	Count %	Statistical record	Monthly
	ii. No. of cases requiring nursing / health care services among total caseload	Count %		Monthly
2. *Outputs measure*	i. No. of outreaching visits	Count	Statistical record	Monthly
	ii. No. of active cases served	Count	Statistical record	Monthly
	iii. Cases turnover rate (No. of closed cases over new / reactivated cases)	%	Statistical record	Monthly
	iv. Duration of closed cases	Count	Statistical record	Monthly
	v. No. of potential cases	Count	Statistical record	Monthly
	vi. No. of new contact cases	Count	Statistical record	Monthly
	vii. No. of group / programmes	Count	Statistical record	Monthly
	viii. No. of health programmes	Count	Statistical record	Monthly
	ix. No. of volunteer training sessions	Count	Statistical record	Monthly

Proposed Performance Indicators for MDTESS (*continued*)

Standard / Criteria	Indicators		Calculation / Formula	Source of Data	Frequency of Data Collection
Effectiveness Perspective					
1. ***Rehouse and reintegrate into the society***	i.	No. of elderly street sleepers rehoused	Count	Statistical record	Monthly
2. ***Improve hygiene*** On a 5-point scale on hygiene	i.	No. of cases improved by 4 points and % among total no. of cases	Count %	Case Assessment Form I (CAF I) (monthly updating)	End of period (Quarterly then)
	ii.	No. of cases improved by 3 points and % among total no. of cases	Count %	CAF I (monthly updating)	End of period (Quarterly then)
	iii.	No. of cases improved by 2 points and % among total no. of cases	Count %	CAF I (monthly updating)	End of period (Quarterly then)
	iv.	No. of cases improved by 1 point and % among total no. of cases	Count %	CAF I (monthly updating)	End of period (Quarterly then)
	v.	No. of cases having no change and % among total no. of cases	Count %	CAF I (monthly updating)	End of period (Quarterly then)
	vi.	No. of cases deteriorated by 1 point and % among total no. of cases	Count %	CAF I (monthly updating)	End of period (Quarterly then)
	vii.	No. of cases deteriorated by 2 points and % among total no. of cases	Count %	CAF I (monthly updating)	End of period (Quarterly then)
	viii.	No. of cases deteriorated by 3 points and % among total no. of cases	Count %	CAF I (monthly updating)	End of period (Quarterly then)

Proposed Performance Indicators for MDTESS (*continued*)

Standard / Criteria	Indicators		Calculation / Formula	Source of Data	Frequency of Data Collection
	ix.	No. of cases deteriorated by 4 points and % among total no. of cases	Count %	CAF I (monthly updating)	End of period (Quarterly then)
3. *Maintain communication with helping professionals* On a 5-point scale on clients' attitude towards MDTESS staff	i.	No. of cases improved by 4 points and % among total no. of cases	Count %	CAF I (monthly updating)	End of period (Quarterly then)
	ii.	No. of cases improved by 3 points and % among total no. of cases	Count %	CAF I (monthly updating)	End of period (Quarterly then)
	iii.	No. of cases improved by 2 points and % among total no. of cases	Count %	CAF I (monthly updating)	End of period (Quarterly then)
	iv.	No. of cases improved by 1 points and % among total no. of cases	Count %	CAF I (monthly updating)	End of period (Quarterly then)
	v.	No. of cases having no change and % among total no. of cases	Count %	CAF I (monthly updating)	End of period (Quarterly then)
	vi.	No. of cases deteriorated by 1 points and % among total no. of cases	Count %	CAF I (monthly updating)	End of period (Quarterly then)
	vii.	No. of cases deteriorated by 2 points and % among total no. of cases	Count %	CAF I (monthly updating)	End of period (Quarterly then)
	viii.	No. of cases deteriorated by 3 points and % among total no. of cases	Count %	CAF I (monthly updating)	End of period (Quarterly then)
	ix.	No. of cases deteriorated by 4 points and % among total no. of cases	Count %	CAF I (monthly updating)	End of period (Quarterly then)

Proposed Performance Indicators for MDTESS (*continued*)

Standard / Criteria	Indicators		Calculation / Formula	Source of Data	Frequency of Data Collection
4. *Strengthen understanding of community resources*	i.	Among cases not receiving but assessed to be in need of accommodation services:			
	a)	No. and % of cases who understood the service after its introduction	Count %	Case Assessment Form II (CAF II) (quarterly updating)	End of period (Quarterly then)
	b)	No. and % of cases who did not understand the service after its introduction	Count %	CAF II (quarterly updating)	End of period (Quarterly then)
	ii.	Among cases not receiving but assessed to be in need of nursing / health care service:			
	a)	No. and % of cases who understood the service after its introduction	Count %	CAF II (quarterly updating)	End of period (Quarterly then)
	b)	No. and % of cases who did not understand the service after its introduction	Count %	CAF II (quarterly updating)	End of period (Quarterly then)
	iii.	Among cases not receiving but assessed to be in need of personal care services:			
	a)	No. and % of cases who understood the service after its introduction	Count %	CAF II (quarterly updating)	End of period (Quarterly then)
	b)	No. and % of case not understood the service after introduction	Count %	CAF II (quarterly updating)	End of period (Quarterly then)
	iv.	Among cases not receiving but assessed to be in need of CSSA / Financial assistance:			
	a)	No. and % of cases who understood the service after its introduction	Count %	CAF II (quarterly updating)	End of period (Quarterly then)

Proposed Performance Indicators for MDTESS (*continued*)

Standard / Criteria	Indicators	Calculation / Formula	Source of Data	Frequency of Data Collection
	b) No. and % of cases who did not understand the service after its introduction	Count %	CAF II (quarterly updating)	End of period (Quarterly then)
	v. Among cases not receiving but assessed to be in need of counselling services:			
	a) No. and % of cases who understood the service after its introduction	Count %	CAF II (quarterly updating)	End of period (Quarterly then)
	b) No. and % of cases who did not understand the service after its introduction	Count %	CAF II (quarterly updating)	End of period (Quarterly then)
	vi. Among cases not receiving but assessed to be in need of other services:			
	a) No. and % of cases who understood the service after its introduction	Count %	CAF II (quarterly updating)	End of period (Quarterly then)
	b) No. and % of cases who did not understand the service after its introduction	Count %	CAF II (quarterly updating)	End of period (Quarterly then)
5. *Enhance motivation to receive services*	i. Among cases not receiving but assessed to be in need of accommodation services:			
	a) No. and % of cases who accepted the service after the introduction	Count %	Case Assessment Form II (CAF II) (quarterly updating)	End of period (Quarterly then)
	b) No. and % of cases who declined the service after its introduction	Count %	CAF II (quarterly updating)	End of period (Quarterly then)
	ii. Among cases not receiving but assessed to be in need of nursing / health care services:			

Proposed Performance Indicators for MDTESS (*continued*)

Standard / Criteria	Indicators	Calculation / Formula	Source of Data	Frequency of Data Collection
	a) No. and % of cases who accepted the service after its introduction	Count %	CAF II (quarterly updating)	End of period (Quarterly then)
	b) No. and % of cases who declined the service after its introduction	Count %	CAF II (quarterly updating)	End of period (Quarterly then)
	iii. Among cases not receiving but assessed to be in need of personal care services:			
	a) No. and % of cases who accepted the service after its introduction	Count %	CAF II (quarterly updating)	End of period (Quarterly then)
	b) No. and % of cases who declined the service after its introduction	Count %	CAF II (quarterly updating)	End of period (Quarterly then)
	iv. Among cases not receiving but assessed to be in need of CSSA / Financial assistance:			
	a) No. and % of cases who accepted the service after its introduction	Count %	CAF II (quarterly updating)	End of period (Quarterly then)
	b) No. and % of cases who declined the service after its introduction	Count %	CAF II (quarterly updating)	End of period (Quarterly then)
	v. Among cases not receiving but assessed to be in need of counselling services:			
	a) No. and % of cases who accepted the service after its introduction	Count %	CAF II (quarterly updating)	End of period (Quarterly then)
	b) No. and % of cases who declined the service after its introduction	Count %	CAF II (quarterly updating)	End of period (Quarterly then)

Proposed Performance Indicators for MDTESS (*continued*)

Standard / Criteria	Indicators	Calculation / Formula	Source of Data	Frequency of Data Collection
	vi. Among cases not receiving but assessed to be in need of other service:			
	a) No. and % of cases who accepted the service after its introduction	Count %	CAF II (quarterly updating)	End of period (Quarterly then)
	b) No. and % of cases who declined the service after its introduction	Count %	CAF II (quarterly updating)	End of period (Quarterly then)
Equity Perspective				
1. *Wide sources of referrals*	i. No. and % of case referrals by MDTESS-initiated outreaching	Count %	Statistical record	Monthly
	ii. No. and % of case referrals informed by public	Count %	Statistical record	Monthly
	iii. No. and % of case referrals by other service units / welfare agencies	Count %	Statistical record	Monthly
	iv. No. and % of case referrals by other sources	Count %	Statistical record	Monthly
Quality Perspective				
1. *Service quality*	i. No. and time schedule of outreaching sessions per week		Agency record	
	ii. No. of escort service	Count	Statistical record	Monthly
	iii. Types and no. of groups (sessions) / programmes	List types Count	Statistical record	Monthly
	iv. Total attendance / Average attendance per group session / programme	Count Mean	Statistical record	

Proposed Performance Indicators for MDTESS (*continued*)

Standard / Criteria		Indicators	Calculation / Formula	Source of Data	Frequency of Data Collection
	v.	Types and no. of health care programmes	List types Count	Statistical record	Monthly
	vii.	Total attendance / Average attendance per health care programme	Count Mean	Statistical record	Monthly
	viii.	Types and no. of concern visits	List types Count	Statistical record	Monthly
	ix.	Total no. of street sleepers visited / Average no. of street sleepers visited per visit	Count Mean	Statistical record	Monthly
	x.	Among the programmes / visits involving volunteers: Total attendance of volunteers / Average attendance of volunteers per programme / visit	Count Mean	Statistical record	Monthly
	xi.	Total attendance of volunteers in volunteer training programmes / Average attendance of volunteers per training sessions	Count Mean	Statistical record	Monthly
	xii.	No. of compliments received from clients / referrals	Count	Agency record	
	xiii.	No. of compliments received from volunteers	Count	Agency record	
	xiv.	No. of complaints received from clients / referrals	Count	Agency record	
	xv.	No. of complaints received from volunteers	Count	Agency record	

Proposed Performance Indicators for MDTESS (*continued*)

Standard / Criteria	Indicators	Calculation / Formula	Source of Data	Frequency of Data Collection
2. *Management quality*	i. No. of supervision sessions for staff	Count	Agency record	
	ii. No. of staff meetings	Count	Agency record	
	iii. Documentation on operational guidelines, case records, staff records, etc.		Agency record	
	iv. Financial management:			End of period
	a) Breakdown of actual cost against estimated breakdown cost		Financial account record	
	b) Compliance with account procedure		Agency record	
3. *Staff quality*	i. No. of qualified staff		Agency record	

11

Organizational Change: Case Analysis on the Formation of Integrated Team for Youth Service

HO Wing Cheung, Andy

Introduction

In response to the movement of service integration and increasing demands on service accountability in the welfare field of Western societies, service provisions of youth work are expected to have tremendous changes on the public, the Government and the non-governmental organizations in Hong Kong.

In the "White Paper: Social Welfare into the 1990s and Beyond", it was stated that "In view of the changing needs of the young there is a need to review the mode of operation of children and youth centres to maximize their contribution to the overall development of the young."[1] The Working Party on Review of Children and Youth Centre Services was appointed by the Secretary of Health and Welfare in March 1992. After a lengthy deliberation, it was concluded that "while overseas experience provided helpful reference, Hong Kong needs to develop its own model on delivery of service for children and youth."[2] Ten Integrated Teams based at children and youth centres were recommended to be set

---

[1] White Paper: Social Welfare into the 1990s and Beyond, Hong Kong Government, March 1991.

[2] Report on Review of Children and Youth Centre Services, Hong Kong Government, 1994.

up at the initial stage to examine this new service model integrated approach in delivering youth services.

Being one of the largest youth service organizations in Hong Kong, the Review set up two Integrated Teams with the support of the Department in January 1994. This paper tries to serve as an organizational studies identifying the important management issues for the formation of one of the teams and to analyze its contextual environment. The theoretical construction of Competing Values Model is applied as the basic analytical framework for studying the organizational issues. Further strategic objectives will be formulated at the end of the paper.

Throughout this paper, the Integrated Team itself is treated as an organization which of course operates under the auspices of its mother organization. An organizational change is defined as the changing process from an existing mode of operation to the Integrated Team.

Background

In the district, the Agency operates several youth service units under the conventional mode of operations, namely, three children and youth centres, one outreaching social work team, school social work service in one family life education unit and a non-subvented indoor centre. To establish the Integrated Team, the resources of the outreaching social work team are pooled together in a major youth service unit in a catchment area with a population size of 60,000. The Team is assumed to provide integrated youth services for the catchment.

Thirteen social work staff and five supportive staff are deployed for the Team. Among them, more than one half of the staff come from the children and youth centre and the outreaching social work team, while the remaining staff are deployed from other service units outside the district or newly recruited. The Team is supervised by one supervisor.

Problem Identification: Existing Mode of Operation and its Problems

Before going into the details of the Integrated Team, it is essential to review the experience of the Agency's youth services under the existing mode of youth service in the district and to identify the basic elements of the integrated service mode.

According to the "White Paper: Social Welfare into the 1990s and Beyond", under the welfare programme, children and youth services are delivered mainly through children and youth centres, outreaching social work and school social work.[3] However, there are limitations of such a kind of service delivery system. The problems of each category of service and the overall service system are presented in the following session.

1. Children and youth centres

It mainly targets at the "normal youth" in the community with balanced activities to fulfill the developmental needs of young people. Social workers apply the techniques of social groupwork to organize the young people so as to develop their potential and ability to the greatest extent. Though the programmes are expected to be designed to be in accord with the needs of the local community,[4] no special planning mechanism has been applied clearly to cater for the community needs, and centre staff are always found to be positive and responsive to the youth needs in the community.

2. Outreaching social work service

The service mainly seeks to reach out to targets of the "marginal youth" in working spots in the community. Social workers are to provide counselling guidance and other services to help them overcome their problems, maximize their potential and become socially reintegrated.[5] A clear labelling of the group as socially maladjusted creates a strong stigmatization effect. Targets are seldom integrated into clienteles of centre services, and they are expelled by the adult world.

---

[3] See note 1, p. 27.
[4] p. 27.
[5] See note 1, p. 28.

3. School social work service

The service mainly assists those students at risk in solving their personal problems and to make maximum use of their educational opportunities for adulthood.[6] Due to the stringent manning ratio of one social work staff to more than two thousand students, the service can only provide a remedial function in school. Social workers always employ techniques with a problem oriented working approach to serve those with problems. Such a kind of working relationship creates negative effects on those students who seek help from the social worker. It is important to take care of the developmental needs of most other students to the interest of the school.

4. Overall service delivery system

As a service delivery system for youth work, it is experienced that the services are fragmented and less responsive to the current needs of the youth. The three services are rigid in service boundary, reaching only certain groups of young people with special needs or problems. An over-generalized classification approach has been employed to look at young people; they can only be classified into "normal youth", "marginal youth" and "youth at risk". It is assumed that youth problems can be relieved through such a kind of fragmented service system. In fact, there are many service gaps for those outside this classification framework, for example, the majority silent who suffer from great pressure under the education system of Hong Kong. New perspectives of service provision is deemed necessary not only to meet the current needs of young people today but also to review the working relationship among the social work staff under the existing rigid service mode.

Some important managerial problems are obvious under the existing mode of service, which should be catered for in the new service mode. Firstly, the nonexistence of formal communication among the service

---

[6] See Note 1, p. 28.

units and their staff discourages the sharing of information of their working experience. Secondly, flexible deployment of financial and human resources is not allowed under the constraint of subvention policy. Thirdly, the high division of work among the three working approaches makes the youth work more fragmented through the specialization process. Coordination in service delivery and in the planning process cannot be achieved, which in turn makes the overall service system not responsive to the total needs of young people in the community.

Concept of Integration Revisited

The direction of horizontal integration is clearly spelled out in the "White Paper: Social Welfare into the 1990s and Beyond":

> "an integration approach of service delivery will help to overcome the difficulties created by the compartmentalizing of clients' needs and the fragmenting of service provision. Such an approach will provide clients with a more convenient access to a wide range of services and enable more flexible and cost-effective use of available resources... There are valid grounds for greater integration of welfare services for children and youth, combining the current provision of children and youth centres, outreaching social work and school social work with a view to provide a comprehensive range of services by the same agency on a geographical basis... Integration in this area will focus on the total needs of young people".[7]

Although the definition of integration is not the focus of this paper, it is necessary to lay down some of its important considerations for the formation of the Integrated Team. Integration is not merely the sum of its parts. It serves to relieve the generic problems in service delivery of fragmentation, inaccessibility, discontinuity and unaccountability.[8]

[7] Ibid., p. 48.

[8] Agranoff, Robert. "Services integration". In Kramer, R.M. and Specht, H. (eds.) *Readings in Community Organization Practice*. Engelwood Cliffs, NJ: Prentice-Hall, 1983, p. 331.

Developing New Service Model for Integrated Team

For the formation of the Integrated Team, it is essential to work out a new service model for the operation of the Integrated Team. An attempt has been made to identify the major managerial issues of the Team in this paper. The Competing Value Model is applied as a conceptual framework for studying the contextual analysis of the Team.

The Competing Values Model, as stated by Robert E. Quinn, provides a comprehensive analytical framework to study the complex and dynamic organizations that are settings in which managers must fulfill many competing expectations.[9] The framework starts with a cognitive map (Fig. 1) which suggests the consideration of two competing variables of flexibility versus control and external focus versus internal focus.

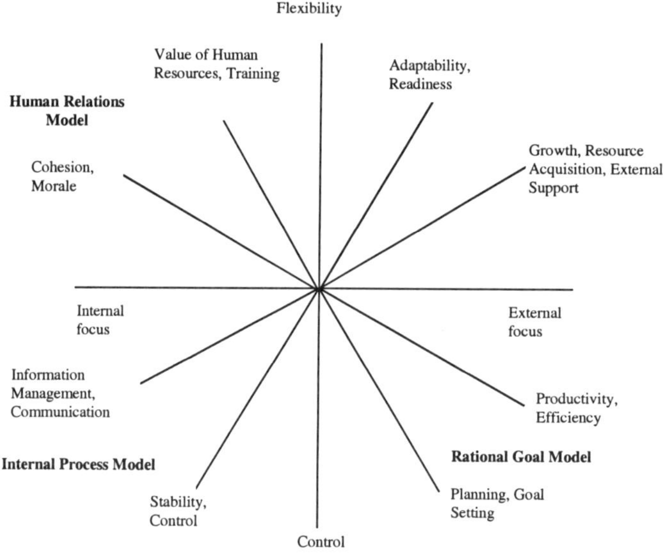

Fig. 1. Competing Value Model framework.
Source: Adapted from Quinn (1988), Fig. 5 (p. 48)

[9] Quinn, Robert E. *Beyond Rational Management Mastering the Paradoxes and Competing Demands of High Performances.* Jossey-Bass Publishers, 1988, p. 45.

Four quadrants representing four major models in organization theory are created. They are the human relations model which aims at human commitment; the open systems model which aims at expansion and adaptation; the rational goal model which aims at maximization of output and the internal process model which aims at consolidation and continuity. The essence of the Competing Values Model is to redefine organizational effectiveness as well as change, to allow managers to have the capacity to see problems from contradictory frames and to entertain and pursue alternative perspectives.[10] The four competing models indeed provide a clear base for studying the contextual analysis for formulating the management issues of the Integrated Team.

In this paper, it is attempted to analyze the crucial management issues of the Integrated Team by examining its contextual situations based on the Competing Values Model framework. The issues evolve from the different considerations which are contradictory to each other alongside the two variables of internal focus versus external focus and flexibility versus control.

Methodology of Study

To study the management issues of the Integrated Team, information is mainly obtained from individual interviews with staff to be posted to the Integrated Team, literature review and reviewing of policy papers, and through reflection of personal experience.

Before going into the details of the study, it must be noted that there are some limitations or characteristics of this study. Although the Competing Values Model framework applies to the study of the various competing dimensions of the organization, great emphasis is placed on the human factors of the organization. For example, much of the information is obtained from the staff's perspective or from their own points of view. The reason for such an emphasis is due to the great importance of staff involvement and their commitment in the process of formation of the Integrated Team.

---

[10] Ibid. p. 45.

Contextual Analysis of Formulation of Management Issues of the Integrated Team

An intensive study on the contextual environment has been made and the following session tries to identify some of the major management issues based on the four quadrants of the Competing Values Model.

1. Human Relations Model quadrant

To start with the organizational analysis, an attempt to have individual discussions with all staff who have been appointed to the positions of the Integrated Team has been made to explore their perception on the formation of the Team. Among the staff, most of those who are deployed from the existing service units have been working in the Agency for more than two years. Those newly recruited have also been working in the youth work field for no less than two years before joining the Team. It can therefore easily be concluded that these experienced staff, who have been well informed in advance that they will be posted to the Team, should be well prepared to adapt to this organizational change. However, it is surprising to learn from the staff that they are psychologically not well prepared for the transition.

There are some similar responses from them. Firstly, during the discussion it is noted that they stick firmly to the perspective of their previous working experience. For example, those who have been working in a centre service always perceive the service as well planned and scheduled systematically. They stick to the concept of centre base which assumes that the youth will join the service in the centre. However, the outreaching social workers strongly request to have flexible and spontaneous intervention techniques and working habits. Meanwhile, the school social workers are used to maintaining the microscopic view on human service and their problem oriented approach in service delivery. Secondly, as the staff are uncertain about the change, their response is just to "wait and see". They are not ready to voice out their own expectations of the new arrangements. Thirdly, besides uncertainty, there is anxiety among them simply because they have very limited understanding of the working conditions of those services out of their experience. Due to their limited experience on casework, groupwork or organizing large scale activities, they face the transition of technology job-fit from a specialization to a generalization approach. It is obvious that there is a common ground for such reactions from staff. The staff lack the knowledge and skills in a wide spectrum of youth services since they are used to fixing their working approach on one of the existing service settings.

Further to the specialization of the working approach, the high rigidity on the division of work discourages the spirit of team work. As discussed with the staff, it is observed that their working habits, no matter whether or not they are from centre services, outreaching social work or school social work, require them to provide their service by their own effort. Team building is not the main focus of their daily work, especially among different working settings. Conflicts and mistrust even sometimes occur because they cannot share a common understanding of the working method. For example, some centre staff always complain about the outreaching social workers' bringing in of marginal youth which affects the image of the centre in the community. Moreover, the school social workers sometimes reject extending service in their schools as they are worried that the centre staff will overshadow their role in the school. For the formation of the Integrated Team, the two important human relations issues to be attended to are the cultivation of an attitude for change which motivates the staff to adapt to the drastic change of working from the specialization to the generalization approach, and the development of team building which is essentially important to be cultivated among the staff who have rich experiences in their specialized and fragmented fields of service settings.

2. Open System Model quadrant

According to the Report on Review of Children and Youth Centre Services, an integrated team would be set up for a catchment area with a youth population of 12,000 in a densely populated district.[11] The role of the integrated team in a community has been clearly defined: "The

---

[11] See note 2, p. 37.

major or even the only youth service unit in the community, integrated team should have the mission in devising strategies to respond and address to the local youth needs, to arouse the community's concern over youth-related issues so that young people could grow up in a more concerned and supportive environment".[12] The concept of community based service provision has been clearly spelt out.

However, with a view of formulating the community needs analysis with the staff who have been working in the community, it was astonishing to find out that they are not well informed about the community issues and youth problems in the catchment area. They have very limited understanding of the resources available, expectation of residents in the catchment area on service provisions for young people, influence and contribution of the District Board or other community organizations on youth issues, and even the competition of youth services in the community. After further discussion with the staff, it is resolved that this phenomenon occurs due to the fragmented approach in service delivery in which social workers only attend to individual aspects of their client system profile but neglect the full picture of youth profile in the community. Thus, for adapting to the organizational change, it is essential to fill the gap between the demand on youth services from the community on the one hand and the lack of a comprehensive community oriented working approach for the staff team on the other.

Several considerations for the Team are suggested in the following for defining the expansion and boundary of system of the Team. Firstly, there exists a very well defined service boundary or catchment area for the Team, that is, the central area of the district. The population profile, distribution of youth related organizations such as schools, the black spots such as places for selling drugs and psychotropic substances where youth problems arise, and the concerns of youth issues of the political parties in the district are some of the important information to be worked out by the Team in the particular catchment area of the district. Secondly, the positioning and targeting of the

---

[12] Implementation Guide to Report on Review of Children and Youth Centre Services, Hong Kong Government, April 1994, pp. 19–20.

Team are essential to give a clear picture of operation of the Team both to the staff and the community. The marketing technique of segmentation can be applied to ensure that appropriate services are provided to the needy in the community with adequate coordination among the service arms. Thirdly, in view of the ever changing characteristic of community needs, the deployment of resources within the Team should be flexible enough to respond to environmental changes.

The changes may occur due to the general environment, such as the political impact generated when China resumes the sovereignty of Hong Kong, the changing family system and increase of single parent families, the change in relationships among young people as well as the adult world. Moreover, no further resources will be invested in youth services from the Government or from the task environment, such as the competition of similar services in the community, specific youth related issues, changes in community criticism, support, and funding sources. Last but not least, mechanisms for community planning should be created and the community sensitivity of staff should be cultivated during the formation stage of the Team.

3. Rational Goal Model quadrant

It has been discussed that the existing mode of youth work has clearly been split up into centre service, outreaching social work and school social work with a different emphasis on development, preventive and remedial nature in each of these three working approaches. However, it is obvious that the three working approaches share quite similar perspectives on how to perceive young people, the way to define youth problems, and the role of social workers in response to the youths' needs. Then, an interesting question will flow if the three groups of staff work together to form an Integrated Team, that is, what will be the objectives of the Team and its specific working approach?

As described in the previous paragraph, the staff adopt the "wait and see" response towards the operation of the Team. Although they have their own ideas of the new service, they do not ascertain the expectation of the agency and its senior staff in the service. In fact, they simply expect that there will be clear instruction on the service directions and its implementation arrangements. On the contrary, there are only vague and general deliberation on the operational objectives and on the actual provisions of this new service as laid down by the Government policy papers. Thus it is clear that a gap between the policy of the Integrated Team and its actual provision in daily operations exists. It is necessary to clarify the value base of service, to build up some agreed service objective or mission statement, to develop operational or strategic objectives and to implement a mechanism with the full participation of the senior staff and the Team members so as to achieve the mutual understanding of the provision of the Integrated Team. A strategic planning mechanism is recommended for further consideration in the formation of the Team.

Apart from goal setting, the study of leadership function of the team is another important area for its formation stage. As the post of Team leader is taken up by a staff ranked Social Work Officer or Supervisor in the agency, the role of Supervisor in the agency drastically changes. Before the implementation of the Integrated Team, all supervisors of the agency only take on the supervisory role, which focuses on supervising the units-in-charge or the social workers of the units. When the supervisor is deployed to the Team, he must make many adjustments to the role of being the person in-charge of the Team. Besides the supervisory role, he must also be responsible for the administration, service planning, community liaison and even the overall development of the Integrated Team service in the agency. Since the Team is in its formation stage without its own traditions, the Team leader is essentially important as a director assisting the Team in laying down the foundation for its operation. As mentioned above, the Team members lack clear directions and understanding of the concept of the new service. The leader should be sensitive enough to detect the needs of the staff and to initiate the discussion on value clarification, taking on an important facilitator role in the formulation of a strategic plan for the Team.

Although the Team leader should take an active role to initiate the concerted effort of the staff in the formation stage, he cannot be a directive leader as he is working with the professionals who have their own initiatives and professional inspirations. In this new Team, most of the staff are professionally trained and have some working experience before joining the Team. They have their own visions and expectations of the development of this new service. Participatory planning with a balanced concern for people and for the product[13] is recommended.

4. Internal Process Model Quadrant

As stated at the beginning of the paper, the implementation of the Integrated Team is the consequence of the trend of an increasing demand on service accountability and efficiency in the social work field. In line with the policy of the Hong Kong Government to apply the concept of service pledges which is addressed by the Governor Christopher Patten in his policy speech, the Social Welfare Department, which provides the source of funds for non-governmental organizations, has laid down tight monitoring controls in the service of the Integrated Team.

According to the *Implementation Guide to Report on Review of Children and Youth Centre* services, "on [an] annual basis, integrated teams will be in collaboration with the Social Welfare Department to carry out various performance-based evaluation including service agreement, annual work plan, quarterly statistics, half-yearly service review and annual evaluation in which both quantitative and qualitative indicators are essential."[14]

The emphasis of evaluation has been shifted from the quantitative approach, using the number of membership and attendance to the centre as performance indicators, to the qualitative one, in which the more objective indicators of core programmes output and staff input analysis have been introduced in the newly designed quarterly statistical

[13] Russell, P.A., Lankford, M.W. and Grinnell R.M. Administrative Styles of Social Work Supervisors in a Human Service Agency. In Slavin, Simon (ed). *An Introduction to Human Services Management Volume I of Social Administration: The Management of the Social Services*. The Haworth Press, Inc., 1985. p. 153.
[14] See note 12, p. 22.

returns for the Social Welfare Department. Moreover, it is anticipated that the Government has imposed the sole responsibility of handling youth problems within the catchment upon individual integrated teams, which imposes much pressure of accountability on the Team. With the emphasis of service effectiveness in qualitative terms, the non-cybernetic management control is becoming more important as the objectives of youth service are ambiguous and its outputs are not easily measurable, together with effects of interventions not known.[15] All these monitoring mechanisms pose new challenges to the frontline youth workers in the Team as they seldom pay much attention to assess the cost-effectiveness of their service. The introduction of the non-cybernetic control on the operation of social work services requires an adaptive response of formulating appropriate information system and evaluative mechanism by the Team.

Formulation of objectives based on Competing Values Model

According to the above contextual analysis, the following objectives are formulated for further development of the new service model (Fig. 2).

1. To formulate a strategic plan with the full participation of the senior staff and Team members (Rational Goal Model).
2. To prepare for the Team leader to devise a new leadership pattern with reference to the characteristics of the stages of formation of the Team (Rational Goal Model).
3. To provide a staff development programme to equip Team members with adequate knowledge as well as skills in a wide spectrum of youth service provisions to cultivate an attitude for change and to develop the concept of team building (Human Relations Model).

---

[15] Hofstede, Geert. Management control of public and not-for profit activities. *Accounting, Organizations and Society.* **6**(3), pp. 196–197.

4. To devise a community planning mechanism for service planning and to strengthen the community sensitivity of the Team members (Open Systems Model).

5. To build up an appropriate information system and evaluative mechanism to cope with the growing demands on service accountability (Internal Process Model).

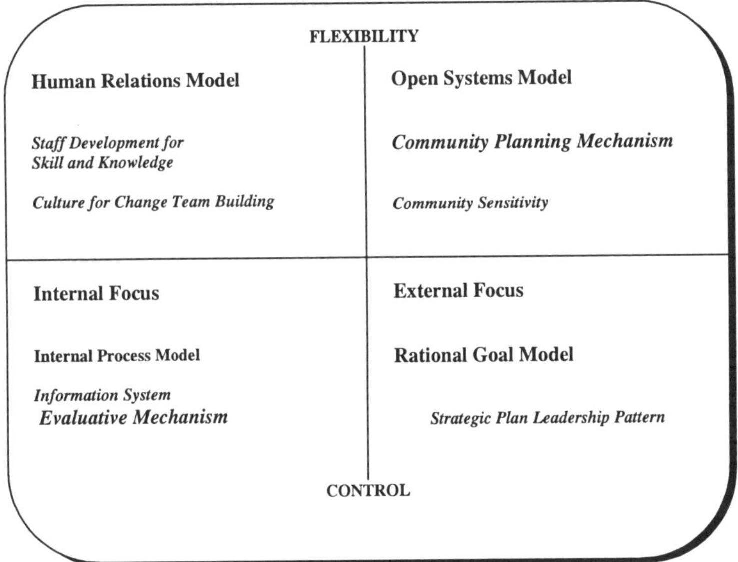

Fig. 2. Objectives formulation for the Integrated Team.

For the time being, the Competing Values Model has laid down a framework for further development of a new service model for the Integrated Team. However, whether or not similar emphasis put on the four models will be a question for further investigation. Perhaps, what Quinn suggested for the four distinctive transitional stages of entrepreneurial, collective, formalization and elaboration stages in the development of new organizations[16] can be useful for the formation of the Team. As recommended, the criteria associated with the open systems

---

[16] See note 9, p. 59.

model and human relations model appeared to be the most important ones for the entrepreneurial stage and collective stages, or the beginning phase of the young organizations. In this connection, these two models of open systems and human relations will be the main concern of the Integrated Team as it is treated as a newly developed organization for discussion purposes.

Looking ahead

It is to be concluded in this workshop paper that the Competing Values Model can provide a systematic framework for studying the organization and to lay down some important objectives for the formulation of a strategic plan for the formation of the Integrated Team. However, the process of formulating the strategic plan, with the conflicts or competing positions of its strategic objectives and the limitations of applying this Competing Values Model, will be further worked out in the implementation stage.

References

Hofstede, Greet. Management control of public and not-for profit activities. *Accounting, Organizations and Society,* **6**(3).

Hong Kong Government (1994) *Implementation Guide to Report on Review of Children and Youth Centre Services.*

Hong Kong Government (1994) *Report on Review of Children and Youth Centre Services.*

Hong Kong Government (1991) *White Paper: Social Welfare into the 1990s and beyond.*

Kramer, R.M. and Specht, H. (1983) *Readings in Community Organization Practice. Engelwood Cliffs,* NJ: Prentice-Hall.

Quinn, Robert E. (1988) *Beyond Rational Management Mastering the Paradoxes and Competing Demands of High Performance.* Jossey-Bass Publishers.

Quinn, Robert E., Faerman, Sue R., Thompson, Michael P., McGrath, Michael R. (1990) *Becoming a Master Manager A Competency Framework.* John Wiley & Sons, Inc.

Slavin, Simon. (1985) *An Introduction to Human Services Management Volume 1 of Social Administration: The Management of the Social Services.* The Haworth Press, Inc.

Viljoen, John. (1991) *Strategic Management: How to Analyse, Choose and Implement Corporate Strategies.* Longman Professional.

12

A Case Study of an Administrator in a Social Service Organization: Morality and Strategy

CHAN Fung-yi, Pauline

Take Time

Take time to Live, it is one secret of success;
Take time to Think, it is the source of power;
Take time to Play, it is the secret of youth;
Take time to Read, it is the formation of knowledge;
Take time for Friendship, it is a source of happiness;
Take time to Laugh, it helps lift one's head;
Take time to Dream, it hitches the soul to stars;
Take time to Worship, it is the highway to reverence.

(Words found in an administrator's office)

It is so interesting and inspiring to re-interpret my "action learning project". The result might not have identified some resolutions for organizational problems, but it provides a starting point to reconsider the significance of process and action orientation in administrative practice.

Chris Argyris makes a strong claim that "Learning is not simply having a new insight or a new idea. Learning occurs when we take effective action, when we detect and correct error." There is always "a new context" requiring relearning in that new context through action implementation (Argyris, 1993). When acting upon a perceived problem, we are conducting an "inquiry" in a fundamental sense originating from the work of John Dewey (1938). Thought and action are intertwined together, proceeding from doubt to doubt-resolution. A mismatch between the expected results and the results actually achieved triggers off doubt which is construed as the experience of a "problematic situation". Such an inquiry becomes organizational when the actor functions as an agent of an organization according to its prevailing roles and rules (Argyris & Schön, 1996).

Paradoxically my learning is derived from my "undoing" of the action project and comparing with the "doing" of action projects of other classmates who try to inquire into the problematic areas to achieve some changes within their organization context. I would elaborate in the following parts my initial learning from undertaking a project of an in-depth interview with an experienced administrator of a welfare agency, how I pick up a theme and construct a model of administration from the pieces of narratives. The learning process does not stop there. During and after the workshop presentation, I integrally look into certain essential and common issues articulated by the classmates and re-evaluate my original paradigm. I acquired new knowledge for action through a reflective dialogue. Lastly, I would summarize some ideas of social service administration as an initial round up of my inquiry project.

My Delight in Choosing the "Right" Administrator

As I did not work in a welfare service organization, I chose to conduct an in-depth interview with an administrator to explore his practical experiences. My choice stemmed from my pre-conditioned limitation that I could not be a part of the operation system. I have readily accepted this "insignificant" limitation and gone on to identify the appropriate subject for interview.

I finally invited Li as my interviewee. He was the Coordinator of the Group and Community Work Unit of a large multi-service organization. I was familiar with him as I had worked under him, though not directly, for less than two years when I was a staff of the community work service. With 23 years of service in the same agency, he proceeded from a centre-in-charge of a youth centre to the present post, supervising 200 staff. He received social work training in college and administration training in post-graduate studies. The agency has had a history of 43 years of service employing a staff force of over 3,800. In summary, the work experience of Li ranged from youth worker, community organizer, staff union's initiator, and middle and top-level administrator.

My choice of interviewee was based on several assumptions about social service administration. First, it is believed that a welfare organization is also a kind of modern bureaucracy with rules and regulations, and hierarchies of structure to coordinate different tasks and operation flow. An organization is a collectivity composed of individuals in the process of organizing: rule making, delegation of power, task negotiation, role identification, boundaries setting, and decision-making. The bigger the size of that collectivity in terms of the number of individuals, the more complex the internal dynamics of organizational operation is supposed to be. A review of Hong Kong welfare organizations suggests that there is a great variety in the scale of operation and nature of services provided. Among the more than 200 organizations, the above-mentioned agency is one of the largest with nearly 300 units providing social work, education, medical, community and hospitality services. How an administrator places himself or herself in that complexity and introduces changes will be an interesting point for diagnosis.

Another assumption of my project is about the nature of social work knowledge. The length of practice implies a history of real life experience in a specific organizational context. To derive insights from direct work practice, the social worker requires a long time for meaningful cultivation, reflecting and doing, culminating new ideas and integrating multiplicity. Social welfare administration involves interfacing among systems. For example, in the Contingency Model (Glisson,1985), the managerial subsystem interacts with the different subsystems of goals and values, psycho-social, technology, structure and supra-system of external environment. There can be an artful fit of tasks, organizations and people, but there cannot be strict empirical studies and experimentation to scientifically consolidate such a knowledge base. It is in the process of administrative intervention that the actor will interpret the significance of certain events, identify his or her role and evaluate the effectiveness of that managerial action. The senior practitioner is assumed to be more capable of giving a vivid description of his or her attempts and problems as well as explaining the rationale and wisdom behind them.

My last concern was that the moral quality of an administrator is the basic core for human service organization. Such a perspective originates from the philosophical understanding that social work is an existential search for "authenticity" (Taylor, 1992) and administration is an articulation of the moral source. Through the implementation of action and cooperation with others, the administrator translates his morality into a concrete organizational situation. As stressed by Weiner, M.E. (1982), "one of the fundamental and generic values of human services management must be the centrality of human as beings .... the dominance of being-oriented values over thing-oriented values" (Weiner, 1982). Administration is not for the power, but is directed towards the fulfillment of "beingness" (Heidegger, 1956). It is through authentic administration that the human and physical resources are transformed into quality services to the people and their essence as respectable beings are realized. In due process, the administrator cultivates himself or herself into a genuine subject as well.

The Competing Values Model (Quinn, 1988) has pointed out that the administrator is placed in an intersection of flexibility-control and internal-external competing orientations. What the model suggests is flexibility in an organizational role, and the philosophy of openness, cooperation, creativity and innovation. The sectors of organizational activity of human relations, internal process, open system and rational goal models embody distinctive criteria of organizational effectiveness (Edward & Austin, 1991). It is the managerial leader's calibre to master the given paradoxes and dynamically work towards an integrative framework (Quinn, 1988). That capacity, in my point of view, should be generated by an ethical concern to actualize one's "beingness".

Even as the interviewee of my project is an honest, sincere, and caring person, and he seems so articulate about his work ethics, I tell myself that he is the appropriate person for discussing his values in practice.

A Smooth Process of Data Collection and Analysis

Interviews with Li involved moments of trust and sharing. Two in-depth interviews were conducted, one in the staff canteen and the other in his office. For the first contact, I proposed some open-ended questions such as "Would you tell me some impressive episodes in your career as an administrator?", "What kind of special problems have you encountered?", "Do you find a sense of achievement in the process and how would you account for that?". I thought he was an expressive man willing to verbalize his opinions. I would regard the first interview as an attempt to understand more about the administrator as a person and his readiness to share his experiences in the agency. I expect to draw a sketch of his perception of the environmental context and some characteristics of his managerial practice. He gave a detailed account of his working life since he first served the organization.

Two major lines of thought were observed. One was his moral vision of commitment and courageous breakthrough. He asserted that "Who[ever] knows the way shows the way and leads the way." A good administrator should not merely follow instructions but should bring forth the staff's commitment to improve and to change for the better. He made that comment right after we started the conversation. He gave a lively description of his hard efforts to work in a tough environment, and his concern for the vulnerable grassroots. A leader was portrayed as a "light" to illuminate and solve problems.

The second point made concerned his intermediate position between the subordinate staff and the upper management. His caring for the staff was demonstrated in his direct involvement in problem-solving with the subordinates, striving for improvement in staff welfare policies and negotiating with the central authority to support the staff's initiatives. Simultaneously, he understood the functions of rules and rank orders to regulate people's performance. He respected the principle of accountability. He actively sought approval from the divisional head and explained the rationale on paper when dealing with tough cases in staff management. But he would argue with the central administration for a positive response to the staff's request for improving services. He made a special remark, "I am part of the administrative structure, but I stand for the staff." He described himself in a "sandwich" position. He seemed to have a good understanding that he was the central person to transform the tension between the staff and managerial structure into favourable changes.

Along the chronological line of narratives by Li, I tried to organize the main theme of "an administrator working upon the dynamics between the staff and the managerial structure". In the second interview, I explored issues of tension with the top management or other central administrators. He presented several stories about the difficulties of fighting to upgrade the computer system, to expand learning class services for the new immigrant children, and to gain back supervisory power over some junior staff. He stressed on his courage and sense of responsibility to negotiate or confront with the agency's unreasonable outdated practices.

What motivated him to bear the blame of "a disturbing guy" when putting up the changes? He responded instinctively that change is a life philosophy, a key to liberate from the constraint of inertia. The staff should keep an active mind to meet new challenges, while the bureaucracy should be flexible, open and responsive to the changing needs. The axis was to convert the human resource and the structure in a facilitating way to serve the needy clients. In the process, the staff should also experience self development, commitment to organization objectives and life enrichment. Should the structure focus too much on status quo, it should be reformed, and an administrator was to make it more "human" to accept changes. During the interview, I used mainly probing questions to ask for further elaboration and clarification of his terms. He was very sensitive to pick up any event for immediate elaboration.

To shed more light on the analysis, I also made some observation of his working environment, interviewed three staff who had worked closely with Li and reviewed the organization's documents. Posted in his office were the mottoes "be a light, not a judge; be a model, not a critic". His moral concern was again represented on the poster at his front door — "be courageous to speak, act and take responsibility". All these were symbols of meaning to him and he admitted that these are notes of reminder for his personal life and work practice.

I was familiar with the three staff interviewees. Two were supervisors and one was from the general office. All of them were senior staff and have worked with Li for more than eight years. We chatted at the dining table and they each felt free to talk with me about Li. Their common point was that he was an open, caring and supportive boss with a great respect for the staff. They felt their suggestions were valued and they were given strong encouragement to go ahead for service improvement. They enjoyed sharing with him about their work and personal lives. He was not a strategic leader, but had a sincere mind to accept diversities of ideas. It was not his sole talent to lead the way. The main strength of his leadership was his respect for participation so that the staff's motivation and contribution was boosted up. The welfare bureaucracy needed such a kind of courageous person to effect changes, the interviewees said, but they made some marginal remarks that the weakness of his leadership laid in his boldness in initiating constant change actions in relation to the central administration. Sometimes that would add anxiety to the exhausted staff. The frustrations of the bureaucracy were exposed and the staff's attention to the immediate workload was distracted. "But that was his own unique style", so the interviewees tended to accept such a "limitation".

A Venue of Morality: My Initial Construct of Administrative Practice

Based upon the collected data, I realized that a framework of administrative patterns was gradually emerging. The construction of my paradigm was an ontological discussion of how a human service administrator lives through his belief to resolve the conflicts in an organization. At the forefront, man is located in his environmental context and nourished by the pre-given historical significance (Taylor, 1992). Base on Li's and my analysis, I picked out several events of the local history that help shape his moral source. One was the Student Movement in the early 1970s when the indigenous college students participated enthusiastically in social events like the Pao Diao Campaign, a time when Li was an active student union member. Another was the socio-economic deprivation of the general public in the 1970s and he could recall vividly how he made efforts to visit and provide shelter for those typhoon victims in squatter areas during a landslide. Against such a background of social consciousness among the young elite, the new profession of social work provided an anchorage point for the practice of social concern. Li's caring orientation for the grassroots began to formulate. He found a strong identification with the welfare agency which he started to serve, serving the goals of "understanding and concern", respecting the people as "the principal agents of their own lives and destinies". At the time of a more systematic policy planning of welfare service in Hong Kong, he participated in establishing the structures for programme expansion of the agency. To him, administration was the realization of his moral ideal and he played a part to develop it.

I recognized an integration of the different roles within one person — a social worker, a community worker, a Catholic, an administrator, and a citizen — the synthesizing force derived from the morality of the man to cultivate his "lifeworld". Li said he had tried to live through his belief, not by spoken words but by action. Such ethical concerns orientated his assessment of the inherent tension between the staff and the administrative structure. He realized the dialectical relationship of facilitation and constraint.

To Li, the structure of a welfare service organization carries the responsibility to serve the people. Its policies and rules are designed to spell out the expectation of that collective entity and to give direction to the members involved as well as the mechanism to facilitate changes for better service to the needy. The staff's motivation and commitment constitute the positive function of the structure. Within the large service unit Li was directly responsible for, he made full use of the structure to encourage the staff's initiatives. When there were promotion posts, he regarded them an incentive to motivate those senior staff who suffered from job fatigue and role fixation. But he negotiated a longer probation period to see if there was significant improvement in job performance. He also initiated a policy of job rotation for those with five or more years of service to apply for a new posting of the same rank in another unit. It was practised as an annual exercise. He believed one should receive adequate stimulation for good performance and the old routine or interpersonal relationship might obstruct to progress.

Li favoured the establishment of the new structure in his large unit to delegate power and achieve collective consensus. He initiated a workers' union to strive for welfare benefits, for instance, to mobilize concern for the annual leave entitlement of the amah. A staff conference was developed as an important platform to discuss the need of pioneering projects for the women, working youth and grassroot resident organizations. He opened up the channel to collect community information through the conference meetings. Whatever new service needs the staff have identified, he readily compiled them into a concrete proposal and applied for financial resources successfully. The structure of the staff conference was governed by democratic rules that the committee members be elected by the staff. Li also proposed to discuss about administrative affairs, for example on the issue of provident fund options. A task group was formed to study welfare policy, and the staff collectively sent letters to the central management to raise questions and demand for changes. Li then affirmed their opinions in other formal meetings in the presence of upper management officials.

Beyond the boundary of his directly supervised units, there was the domain of external environment within the organization context. The related persons widely range from the division head, the executive, board of management, and functional committee to the coordinators of other social services. He analyzed that problems arise when the structure was anchored by people's strong attachment to the power status quo and the associated sense of insecurity upon changes. When the structure became an inflexible system confining the initiatives of the staff, he would position himself as a representative to confront the "adversaries" and query the justification of such a limitation.

A large welfare organization is also a bureaucracy consisting of different smaller parts for the purpose of division of labour, expecting each component part to contribute its best to the total sum of organizational output. But sometimes provincial attitude was fermented, signifying clashes of interest among the units. As an example, the head of education service complained that the community centres under Li had provided an overlapping service of induction programme for new Chinese immigrant children. Li confronted the head about the nature of service. He asserted that the community centre would provide comprehensive social services for the immigrant families. He strengthened his point on community need assessment by presenting a letter from the District Office. It invited the community centres to deliver necessary services for the large number of in-coming Chinese immigrants. In addition, he clarified that the age range of their clients should not cover children below 15. In a written letter of nine pages to the head of education service, with copies sent to the personnel at the headquarters, Li apologized for having stepped over his service boundary. The message was actually a challenge to the complaint. Information was provided and justification was spelt out for serving those potentially overlapped target groups. The final negotiation resulted in such a way that the application of the community centres to organize induction programmes for the new immigrant children would be endorsed by the education service head and sent to the Education Department, in a way respecting Li's formal authority within the organization.

My conclusion upon the narratives of Li is briefly summarized as follows. His experience demonstrates that administration can be a practice of a worker's philosophy in life. A genuine respect for people is a central motivating force to seek new changes, including "physical, attitudinal and structural changes". When put into the organization context, the administrator will always find himself or herself in a difficult mediating position between the staff and the managerial structure. The inertia of these two to changes will obstruct responsiveness to clients' need and the staff's development. But changes differ in internal and external environment.

In the area of autonomous control, the administrator can aim at consolidation by establishing new platforms for the staff's participation and making full use of resources provided by the structure, including time, discretion and opportunities, to promote staff welfare. It is a zone of administrative maneuver to generate commitment and increase work morale. But there is always another area outside the direct responsibility of the administrator. Li shows a pattern of communicating the language of the agency mission in the process of negotiation beyond the zone of his direct maneuvre. Accommodating the agency mission into the personal lifeworld is a valuable asset for an administrator. One can better anchor the self with inner stability, to accept living with the tension caused by the competing forces of human relations and managerial control (Edward & Austin, 1991). Simultaneously, the language of mission statements, if appropriatly cited, can serve as a basic common ground for the discussion among divergent and sometimes conflicting opinions.

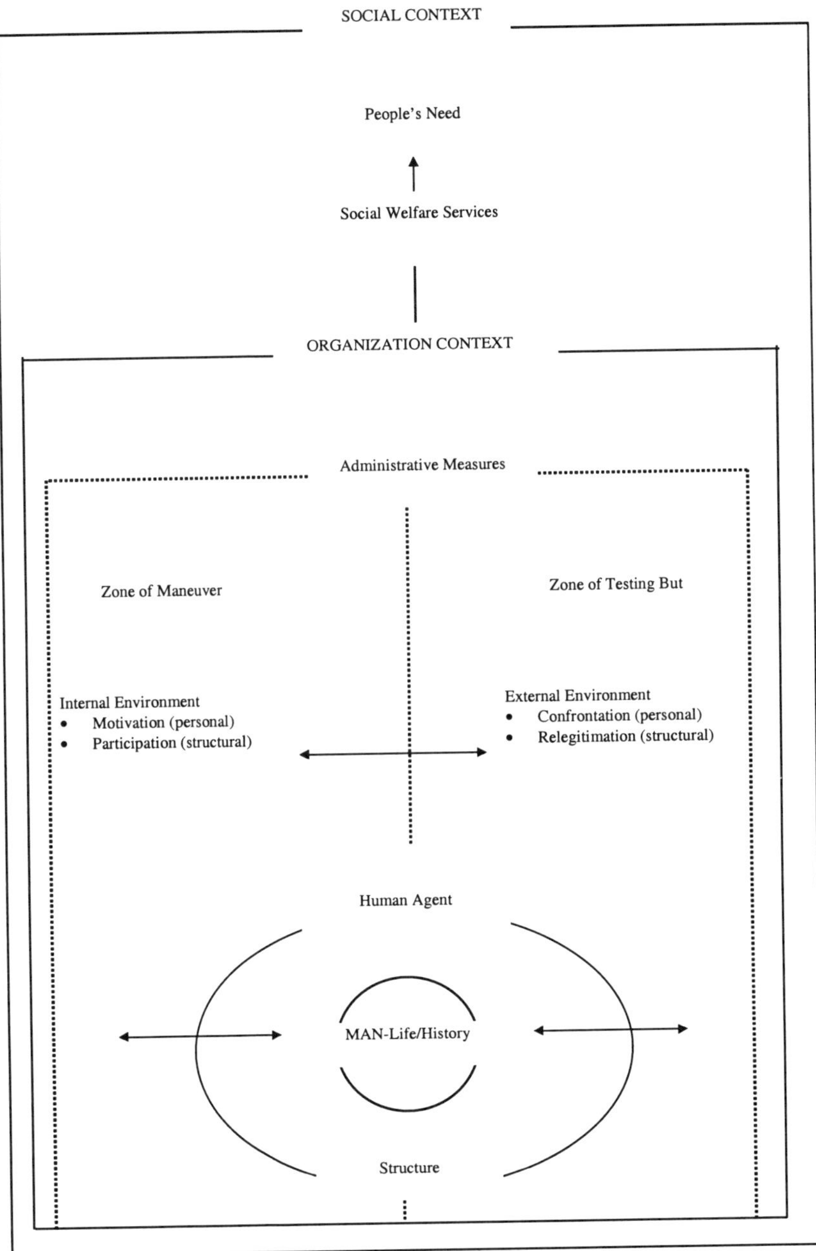

Fig. 1. The administrator in context (life, organization, and social).

The Puzzle from Participation in Group Learning

The two-day workshop on action project presentation gave me insights but the stimulation came after a sense of frustration. The discussion of strategic planning, conflict management, information technology, resource filing, process re-engineering and total quality management seemed to be so different from my ontological version of the moral leadership of Li. When I was enjoying the touching stories of an administrator and trying to appreciate the kind of humanistic leadership being practised in a welfare organization, the difference "discovered" in the discussion strongly alerted me to look deeper. I began to feel uneasy with my original construction.

I remembered a classmate presenting her strategic management in a hospital setting. She raised several meaningful questions which struck my mind: "How do ideas (of change) come out? Is the change feasible, realistic, attainable or specific? Is it a suitable timing for change? How does one get consensus? What is my role and contribution?" Her proposal was situated at a time when the Hospital Authority was attempting total quality management, and hospital services were assessed on the grounds of public accountability as well as operational efficiency. She then presented the design of a strategic planning workshop, how they formulated a mission statement for their medical social services, and how individual staff responded enthusiastically by filling in their opinions properly onto the worksheet at home after a hard day of work stress. In the discussion process, the social workers identified a long list of critical issues and worked out the action plan together. The implementation of the plan would be a long process subject to constant evaluation.

Referring back to my analysis. I wondered whether had Li ever considered the heterogeneity of the staff when getting their consensus over a change proposal. Had he ever come across any difficulties in consolidating the members of his service unit? To what extent did the staff identify themselves with the agency mission, or did they have their own interpretation regarding their specific services? How did he set priorities among the various proposed change actions? How did he assess his role in the change project? Were there any significant discrepancies among his intervention attempts? Did his self-definition of humanistic leadership imply a central proactive position of moral appeal, or an adaptive role to the environment? How did he interpret the learning from the consequences of the different change actions?

The other impressive example from the workshop was the implementation of a computerized reporting system in a family service centre. Against the background of introducing quality standards of welfare services under the recent Subvention Review, the headquarters of the Social Welfare Department was preparing to set up an office to develop information technology. The unit under my coursemate's supervision, however, tried to solve problems on their own because a change in methods was expected to be late and slow in a large department. My coursemate systematically analyzed the existing manual system, SWOT (strength, weakness, opportunity and threat) of the situation, and developed an Information Technology Strategy. He concretely applied the Contingency Model (Glisson, 1985) to look into the psycho-social subsystem of his office. He described how he worked on the anxiety and different emotional responses of the staff, and initiated to share his design and rationale of the action project. The change aroused a motivating atmosphere of learning new computer knowledge among the professional staff and their active participation in working towards the common goal of efficiency, which created team spirit. Such an experience reminded me of Li.

Li shared an account of facing an obstacle in upgrading the computer system of his service. His staff found that the existing computers of the different work units were not capable of processing the data of the members and service output efficiently. There was the wastage of professional manpower for the heavy statistical and paper work. But their application for a financial subsidy of $2,000 per computer was not approved by the equipment vetting committee of the headquarters. The principle of fairness was strictly upheld as the computer systems of all service units of the organization were not yet upgraded. For resource allocation, computerization was not ranked high in the priority list of organization development. Li's service could not be given privileged treatment. The application process lasted half a year and he spent time on writing memos and collecting quantitative information on the needs and problems of the computer system but without any success. Frustrated, he donated the sum of money required to upgrade the computer of his own central office. "We lost the battle, but my colleagues know I am concerned."

Li also made use of the chance to complain about the procrastination in technological renovation. One occurred at the time when his service was required to process the questionnaires of all the staff on the agency's future development. He sharply criticized that the slow process of the data system was due to bureaucratic procedures. Three years later, it was until the introduction of a management audit that Li got another opportunity to raise the same problems. He gave a detailed summary of the computer issue to the auditors and suggested the dissolution of the equipment vetting committee that delayed service improvement.

Compared with the above-mentioned presentation, questions came to mind again. Did Li scan the organization environment and analyze the culture which led to its delay in improving the computer system? Had he ever assessed the timing in view of risk and opportunity factors? If realistically the change action was not successful at the moment, had he ever thought of other alternatives? Had he encouraged the staff to scan the community environment of their respective working area to identify possible resources, like asking for donation of used computers from the community members or local bodies when many people prefer to purchase the latest top models? Did any single office have good experiences in making concerted efforts to upgrade the computer system and install new programmes under the given constraints? Fundamentally, had the administrator ever thought of decentralized problem-solving besides, or instead of, confronting the central bureaucracy for a reform policy when the timing was not suitable?

Rethinking My Thesis of Morality

Puzzles give a shake to original assumptions that promise certainty and a satisfactory explanation. A further thought suggests that Li and I are both constructing a moral ideal in organization administration. It is like a conversation of teaching and learning.

Li was enthusiastic in sharing his work experiences as a kind of life fulfillment, and in explaining the rationale behind his change action in relation to his vision of a human being. His recollection of memories was organized as a thematic account of an authentic being living through his belief. Although the word "problem" was commonly mentioned, the meaning implied was that difficult situations were a testing ground for human courage.

As an interviewer, I found myself in full identification with the moral leader. We had shared a language of "collective participation" and "human autonomy as a liberation from structural constraints". I well understood that it was a big hierarchy, and decision making at the central level seemed to be always a mystery. When Li presented his confrontation with the top management, I was enchanted by his heroic assertiveness in putting forward the proposal from bottom up. My empathy for his venture stems from my genuine respect for those with a deep sense of reflection and the transcendence of the narrow self to a higher order of moral community. Basically I admire those with courage to challenge the authority's unjustified power and who ambitiously act for changes in a bureaucracy. Li's willingness to share with me was always reciprocated by my appreciation to listen.

However, a deeper reflection poses a question: am I trying to formulate a single model of administration to demonstrate the possibility of perfection? The related problem is that I tend not to drill into the context to ask in-depth questions critically. I seem to accept what I am told, accept just to clarify and request for further elaboration. I seem to conduct an outcome analysis and presumed meaning from it. The zig-zag movement of progress and regression is reviewed at a "frozen moment" during the interview, so unlike my classmates' direct experiences. It becomes a story of simple grandeur. When the causal relationship between the moralistic leader (Li) and organizational changes is established, there will be a marginalization of the internal dynamics of the staff, the response of top management and the external dynamics of the environment.

An alternative thought suggests that structural constraint is less imposing than originally assumed. The big organization delegates a high degree of autonomy to Li to manage the sub-structure of his own service unit. The top management can be said to be responsively accommodating to his challenges. Very often when he uses the language of the agency mission to justify his claims, he is actually telling them that he has internalized those values of the organization. Li expressed a sense of pride when he mentioned that the executive head sometimes praised him for showing the agency spirit in his argument for improving the services.

His constant promotion to a higher rank reflects the organization's strong ideology of moral faith and a culture of valuing loyalty. Li was frustrated on certain occasions but also gained recognition and positive reinforcement in many situations. It may be through him and his service staff that the central administrators get the signal of internal problems and environmental changes to which they are insensitive due to their positions.

Similarly, Li's respect for democratic participation of the staff is sustained by an active response of a pool of enthusiastic members, who constantly contribute ideas to changes and support him to test out the power of their collective opinions. It may be understandable that his outspoken character is shaped in a community that such leadership style is treasured and expected. In such a way, his morality is not a pre-given and fixed quality, but a philosophy cultivated in the interaction process between him and the other members of the organization whom he identifies with.

I am not downplaying Li as an active agent to interpret the meaning from the experiences. But I want to supplement that his moral leadership reflects a process of interpersonal negotiation, and a history of organizational evaluation. It is in the dialogue with the people in the organization environment that he draws information to continuously formulate, continue or modify his orientation. That leads to the following discussion of the *possible* relationship between morality, the focus of my analysis and strategy, the concern of my classmates.

Morality & Strategy: A Possible Dialogue?

The mutual construction of moral leadership developed from my interview experience emphasizes the essence of virtue for social service administration. An authentic human being is not only concerned with outcome, but the "qualitative worth" of motivation. A "strong evaluator" can employ a rich language with "contrastive characterization" (Taylor, 1985). As in Li's case, he is articulate about his positioning and choice of actions. His frequent use of words such as "care", "justice", "responsibility", "commitment", and "courage" reflect his belief that moral evaluation is of central importance to him. But does it carry any incompatibility with strategic thinking?

I remembered that during classroom learning, a common concern was brought forth: "What are the basic goals of the change action? How are they related to the changes brought about by social service to the clients?" In strategic planning, such value discussion is also incorporated into elements which include the mission statement, scan of external and internal environment, business strategy statement and integrated programes (Mintzberg, Quinn & Voyer, 1995). For instance, in developing the mission statement, the administrator as well as the staff have to go over an exercise to clarify their value assessment of the clients' needs, the nature of their services and their specific role. In such a process, the assessment goes back to the person's inner self. If an administrator has a deeper sense of self-reflection, he or she will better understand the intrinsic value behind the words and be more committed to the objectives being set.

Ethical concerns also imply an understanding of the context. "Moral decisions are taken in the light of the requirements of a situation and not independently of it ... Moral consciousness signifies my being in a situation, affected by and responding to its requirements" (Michael, 1986). Moral knowledge is generated from historical horizons of understanding, but it should also be translated into a mediation "between the universal and the particular" (Michael, 1986, p. 246). Regarding the particular situation, the "strategy" approach makes a systematic attempt to scan the environment context. *The Executive Guide to Strategic Planning* suggests the assessment of the external opportunities and threats, and the internal strengths and limitations (Below, Morrisey & Acomb, 1987). *The Strategy Process* further puts the concepts of change into different contexts like entrepreneurial, mature, diversified, professional and innovation. (Mintzberg, Quinn & Voyer, 1995). This reminds us that, apart from the primary concern for the administrator as a moral agent, a systematic and detailed scanning of the organization is of equal importance to achieve a more thorough understanding of the complex person-situation interaction.

Strategy as defined by Mintzberg (1995) is "a pattern in a stream of actions over time" (Mintzberg, Quinn & Voyer, 1995, p. 3). His action-oriented approach does not focus mainly on the original "strategic intention". To realize the strategies, we need a combination of both "deliberated" and "emergent" strategies in response to an evolving situation (Mintzberg, Quinn & Voyer, 1995, pp. 15–16). Mintzberg's analysis pinpoints that strategies can "form" as well as be "formulated". Very often the intended plan does not produce the desired action, or the actions do not produce the expected effects. We need a new conception of the relationship between formulation and implementation. We should learn to accept what is emergent. The assumption that thought must be independent of and precede action from an organization's behavior is mistaken. Smart strategists are advised to allow "their strategies to develop gradually, through the organization's actions and experiences", and "appreciate that they cannot always be smart enough to think through everything in advance" (Mintzberg, Quinn & Voyer, p. 112). Prior analysis is thus not for accurate prediction; rather, it serves as an initial framework for further reflection. That sense of conscious evaluation can be a practice of virtue to admit to inescapable shortcomings and strive for betterment.

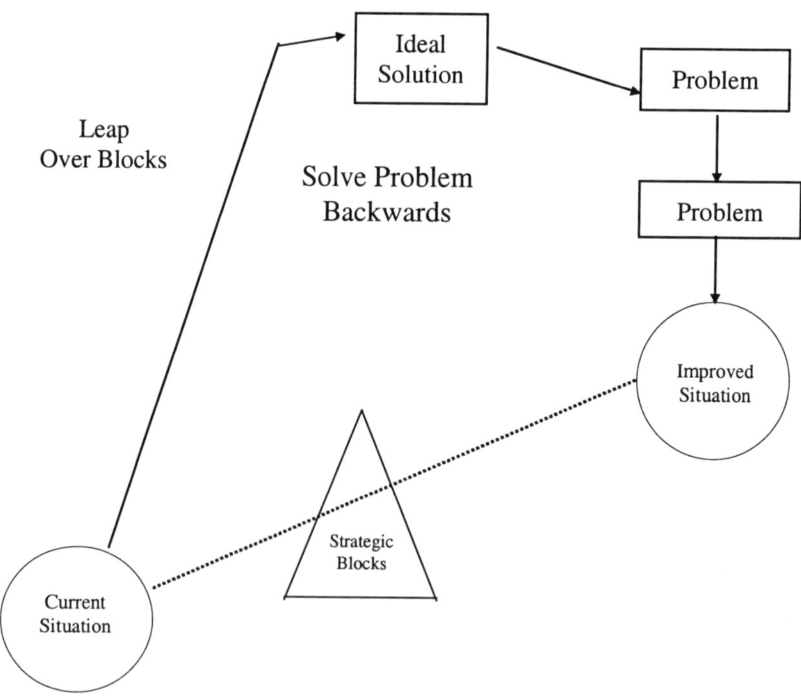

Fig. 2. The Creative Leap (Bandrowski, 1990).

There is always the fallacy of predetermination, and a "strategy" reminds our bounded knowledge in mastering the complete picture. It also highlights the way to move ahead by encouraging creative thinking. Gilbert proposes that "A strategy is simply a set of decisions, the product of thoughtful reflection" (Gilbert, 1992). It also implies a "creative leap" by "jumping to potential idealistic solutions first, then working logically backward to solve the problem in the reverse direction" (Bandrowski, 1990).

Creativity needs imagination and alternative reasonings. In social services, it calls for a wide and wild vision of human development, and an incessant attempt to try a different technology of cultivation in particular scenes. Morality should be grounded on an actual form of realization. As such, creative strategy is the facilitation of moral action in a world of uncertainty.

If I explain the series of "good" actions as the direct result of the moral intention of the actor, am I unconsciously confining myself to the strict boundary of deductive reasoning? When I am concerned about the "practical-moral involvement" (Michael, 1986) of a social work administrator, I almost forget a fundamental orientation as described by the book on "strategy": "The fact is that great art and innovative problem solving require inductive reasoning — that is, the inference of the new general solution from the particular experience" (Mintzberg, Quinn & Voyer, 1995).

The nutrient of creative thinking does not come from a person alone. It is generated from a community. The respect for democratic and collective participation, as illustrated in Li's case is embodied in Charles Taylor's insightful note, "We can coexist only if we have this capacity to reach out and feel the force of one another's moral views, gain a real respect for each other, and develop a comradeship that will serve the program" (Taylor, 1994). The "practice wisdom" of all the staff is already a rich resource pool for creative breakthrough. The kind of administrative style is apparently crafted within a collective entity and culture, the effectiveness or success of which is not dependent on an individual force alone. It is related to the reflection of the whole work team towards a desired moral ideal, and cooperative reformulation of the general goal to meet with the specific, emergent requirements.

I think the strategic assessment of the staff's commitment and expertise as an environmental diagnosis is not giving adequate weight to that basic constituent. The total quality management seems to pay a more positive regard to the people within the organization. "TQM is total in the sense that it must involve everyone in the organization, and that this total management approach is about both the systems and a culture which impinges on all the internal detail of working in the organization, that is all of the internal processes" (Morgan & Murgatroyd, 1994). But the management should be guided by a central concern that "resists treatment of self and others as things" (Weiner, 1982). The staff are not instruments for efficiency; they are learning to collaborate and coordinate in a better way to care.

From the classroom discussion, there are common difficulties in a pre-given organization condition. An administrator of different levels will always struggle in a position between the "problematic past" and "uncertain future", mediating the apathetic or demanding upper management with the underperforming or unmotivated subordinates. A grand piece of re-engineering cannot and should not be the solution. It is essential for an administrator to suggest a strategic point to break through the culture of the organization environment, trying to effect some "micro" changes. But the plan should be formed as a consensus from the staff community, or even be a negotiated product of the staff-client dialogue. On one hand, the administrator needs to have a map of the grand plan. Simultaneously, a small localized area to snowball practical changes is the pre-requisite of goal "realization". That strategic point can only be effectively located, I would emphasize, with an understanding of the historicity of the organization context.

In retrospect, while the classmates present the attempt for an action, my presentation depicts a pattern of actions. The requirement for an administrator to cultivate an open attitude does not merely imply a decontextualized human quality. The humble sense of on-going learning embodies a constant reflection on the existing strategic task, its consequences and the emergent new properties of the contextual "reality". It further implies a readiness to re-examine the basic assumptions of oneself and to accommodate adversaries in the action process. From this line of thinking, I have to accept that my interpretation of Li's leadership illustrates just one kind of "fitting" in an organizational practice. The "sovereignty" of the knowledge drawn from his experience can be and should be "relegitimated" in every specific situation (Michael, 1986).

Last Remarks

I want to add some words to my initial assumption of choosing the "right" person for the interview. From the experience, I am again reminded that the complexity of organization environment is not an objective fact, the perception of which depends on the purpose, sensitivity and strategic mind of the evaluator. Even a small sized agency can be an example of a web of complicated inter-personal relationships, whether social or political. The dynamics in the environmental context is also not a constant variable proportional to the organization's scale of operation. In addition, if the length of practice of an administrator implies something important, the moment of reflection signifies something more. We can learn from a senior practitioner not by the measurement of years of service. The core lesson is to understand how an administrator analyses the organization environment, articulates the rationale of his or her position, presents the way to handle problems and culminates with insights from experiences. The enrichment of administrative knowledge comes from both direct action and learning from those with different perspectives and assumptions. We may carry prejudices and distortions unknown to us.

I enjoy the interview with Li which provide so much stimulation and a sincere touch. It is a valuable chance to listen to a very experienced, respectable administrator's work history. Obviously there is an inherent limitation to my understanding. I do not have that same sense of "proximity" and "responsibility" (Whyte, 1991) of the actor in the action process and my exploration is not as systematically structured as a qualitative research. Yet, a special kind of organizational learning is sparked off. My interview is not strictly an organization action, but I have a taste of moving from "single" to "double-loop learning". I learn to reflect on the governing values of my assumptions and by accommodating those with different paradigms of discussion, I expand my horizons and widen my vision of administration. For an administrator to achieve organizational learning, I think one must also learn to figure out "the two feedback loops that connect the observed effects of action with strategies and values served by a strategist" (Argyris, & Schön, 1996).

An administrator may not be just a model, but also be a good critic of himself or herself also. One will be part of the solution if one is aware that he or she constitutes part of the problem.

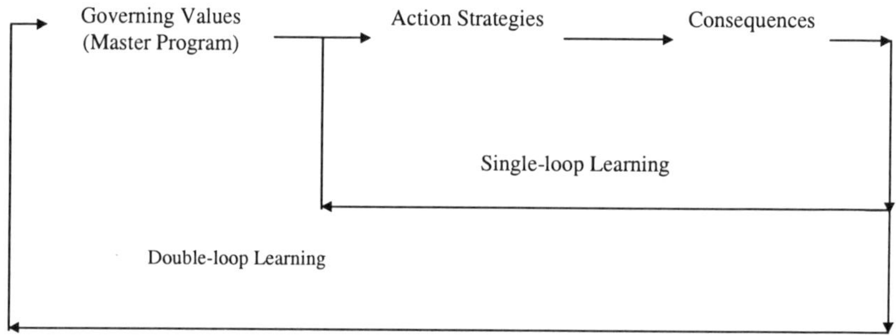

Fig. 3. Single-loop and double-loop learning (Argyris & Schön, 1974).

References

Argyris, C. (1993) *Knowledge for Action*, San Franciso: Jossey-Bass Inc.

Argyris, C. & Schön, D.A. (1996) *Organizational Learning II*, Addison-Wesley Publishing Co. Inc.

Bandrowski, J.F. (1990) *Corporate Imagination Plus*, The Free Press.

Berg, B.L. (1989) *Qualitative Research Methods for the Social Sciences*, Allyn and Bacon.

Bratton, J. & Gold, J. (1994) *Human Resource Management — Theory and Practice*, Macmillan.

Edward, R.L. & Austin, D.M. (1991) *Managing Effectively in an Environment of Competing Values*, in Edwards, R.L. & Yankey, J.A. (ed), *Skill for Effective Human Services Management*, NASW Press.

Gilbert, D.R. (1992) *The Twilight of Corporate Strategy*, Oxford University Press.

Glisson, C.A. (1985) A contingency model of social welfare administration, in Slavin, S. (ed) *Social Administration*, Vol. 1, Haworth.

Mondy, R.W. & Noe III, R.M. (1993) *Human Resource Management*, Allyn and Bacon.

Morgan, C. & Murgatroyd, S. (1994) *Total Quality Management in the Public Sector*, Open University Press.

Quinn, R.E. (1988) *Beyond Rational Management*, San Francisco: Jossey-Bass Inc.

Taylor, C. (1994) *Philosophical Reflections on Caring Practices, The Crisis of Care: Affirming and Restoring Caring Practices in the Helping Professions*, Georgetown University Press.

______, (1992) *The Ethics of Authenticity*, Harvard University Press.

______, (1985) *What is Human Agency, Human Agency and Language*, Cambridge University Press.

The Hong Kong Council of Social Service (1996) *Management of Social Service Agencies: Casebook*.

Weiner, M.E. (1982) The Distinctiveness of Human Services Management, *Human Services Management: Analysis and Application*, Illinois: Dorsey Press.

Whyte, W.F. (1991) *Action Research as Method, Participatory Action Research*, Russell Sage.

Part III
Prologue

13

Impacts of Welfare Reform on Non-Governmental Organizations in Hong Kong: Future Research Agenda

CHAN Kam Tong and Alan Y. H. SZE

Background

This chapter is to trace possible changes on various levels resulting from the introduction of the welfare reform. It covers issues concerning the processes, operation and implementation of the reform to the impacts on various aspects of NGOs across sectors and of different NGO sizes.

This content will not directly assess the detailed operation and implementation of Lump Sum Grant (LSG) and Service Performance Monitoring System (SPMS). Instead it emphasizes the possible impact of these systems on three levels of social service administration: a) macro level, that is the whole welfare system; b) messo level, that is organizational and management responses of the non-governmental organizations; and c) micro level, that is individual players, including service workers, volunteers and users.

Special attention will be paid to service sectors where competitive bidding has been introduced. It is in these sectors where not only has SPMS become an explicit contract monitoring, but also the most unsettling issues concerning contracting arises — forsaken concern over quality, profit (or competitiveness, continued-operation) — orientation, displacement of organizational goals by NGOs, adverse selection of clients and thus deteriorated distributive effect, etc.

Macro Level

Four policy goals are identified for examining the possible impact of subvention reform on system performance: cost-effectiveness, service quality, accountability and relationship.

Cost-effectiveness

Whether there is any gain in cost-effectiveness will be an issue for exploration, by assessing the costs and outcomes through various measurements. Since no baseline study has been conducted in most cases, we expect the comparison on cost would be important while effectiveness indicators have to be constructed to take into account aspects not captured by SQS.

We note that under LSG and SPMS, there is no direct mechanism to ensure cost-effectiveness. It seems to work through the no-claw-back mechanism and the increasing scope of competitive bidding. Besides, although the cost information required to keep and report is more detailed, the figures are in the form of accounting costs.

In the future, we may need a framework developed in another project that is theoretically informed and sound and practically manageable for NGOs of various sizes, for estimating unit cost in social care services in Hong Kong. The aim is to compare the true value of resources expended to provide a given amount of service. Here comes the concept of opportunity cost.[1] Soundly based information about the costs of health and social care services will soon be used in planning and managing of contracts and programme based budgeting.

The framework would be necessary to compare pre and post reform costs within an NGO and among different modes of service provision. When costing information is combined with quantitative (quantifiable outcomes) and qualitative (outcome attributes that are difficult to be expressed in equivalent cost terms) measurements, ordinal ranking and

---

[1] At a macro level, it will involve whether resources should be in the form of private saving and investment or government taxation, and in the domain of public expenditure whether a sum of money should be spent on social care or education or housing, etc.

similar techniques can be employed to judge the change in cost-effectiveness even though there is a lack of a single cost-effectiveness index.

Service Quality

Service Quality Standards (SQS) serves only as a check of minimum standards. These standards are necessarily imperfect and incomplete as to capture all essential aspects of quality services. Thus, one of the crucial concerns in searching the true concepts of quality should be to examine the expectation of service users. Independent and honest feedback from service users would become more and more important so as to ensure service quality.

Accountability

Service Performance Monitoring System (SPMS) and Funding and Service Agreement (FSA) serve as channels through which NGOs have to make themselves accountable to the funders and the public as well as be exposed to greater pressure from them. Whether this is true and to what extent the accountability of NGOs concerns has been improved should be checked through the feedback of heads, workers, volunteers, and users of these NGOs. Recently, corporate governance has become a heated topic in society, both in private and public sector. It is our view that public organizations should be more transparent and accountable to the stakeholders.

Relationship

A. SWD and NGOs

Common and Flynn (1992) identify four models which can be located along the continuum of relationships between parties to a contract, from flexible and trust-based to tightly specified and penalty-based: "partnership" contract and "service agreements" towards the flexible end, "contract manager" and "service contracts" towards the tighter end.

To what extent and in what direction the relationship between SWD and NGOs has been changed due to the subvention reform are questions that could have profound implications on future planning of service provision. Both the SWD and NGO personnel have to examine the new relationship between them.

B. Among NGOs

Competition could lead to fragmentation, compartmentalization and overlap provision of services which are highly inefficient. This can be avoided only when related NGOs maintain not only a non-antagonistic but a partner and collaborator relationship. Tension in terms of competitive bidding while cooperation in terms of sharing of information and resources would certainly create a new agenda among them. The relationship among all the NGOs in the new environment should be further examined.

Messo Level

Financial Management

There are two aspects worth noticing. One concerns salaries and MPF. Since the benchmark is set at the mid-point salary of the recognized establishment plus 6.8% MPF, the financial pressure will be great for agencies with a significant proportion of staff of more experienced workers and those who are promised with more generous retirement benefit packages. In the long run, though the retirement benefit packages can be adjusted with contract renewals, a problem remains due to a stable and maturing team of workers, which might help improve quality above that stipulated in SPMS but not reduce costs.

The second concern will grow with the extension of coverage of contract management to more service sectors. The financial implications for making a successful bidding — though a unit cost but growing requirement for higher quality might imply throat-cutting cost competition — and losing in a tender might be very considerable if not a matter of life and death for an NGO. The incentive and space allowed for income generation might increasingly be active.

It is also from the above background that the other following aspects evolve.

Organizational Goal

It is recognized that different NGOs have their organization goals which distinguish themselves from each other even in providing a similar service. With SPMS and the pressure from tendering, there are concerns about the pressure they will face to put the demands of government defined objectives to beyond the SQS level. The increasing work required to manage contracts will also displace advocacy and development work which very often form the essential components of organization characteristics.

Employment Relationship and Pay Structure

Given that the overall salary structure of NGOs has to follow the mid-point salary of the overall establishment, and since the possibility to renegotiate the overall establishment on agency basis is foreclosed, the only space available for maneuver, apart from revenue generation (fee charging, side-line businesses, donation) and cost-saving, will be the adjustment of the relative pay structure among different ranks. This will change the employment relationship both between experienced and less experienced workers and between the agency and the experienced workers. Directions for the development of a new pay structure can be varied and can affect employee behaviors and employment relationships in polar ways.

Growing attention to competition, cost, and administrative and information management work might also discourage workers who are trained to care and serve and who have less liking towards such work.

Managerial Behavior

Characteristics, members' motivations, capacities and constraints of management committees of NGOs have been demonstrated to have been affected in the UK (Harris, 1997) and elsewhere with the wide introduction of contracts. These include organization growth, pressures to become more accountable and business-like, funding uncertainties and other changes.

Exploratory study of organizations at various stages of negotiation with state bodies can reveal evidence of tensions and difficulties as purchasers and providers struggle to adapt to their changing relationship. Whether or not there will be increased clarity and confidence about their role on the part of the latter should be tested out.

Transaction Cost

Transaction costs incurred by the subvention reform in terms of manpower and time need to be estimated. Areas where transaction costs are likely to be high include: for negotiating terms; for running a contract; increased management information; and increased paper work. In estimating the efficiency of resources allocation, both operating costs and transaction costs should be further examined in the future.

Micro Level

Client Profile and User Feedback

In view of the cost pressure and the quantitative output requirement, it is worth examining whether "cream skimming" occurs after the welfare reform and using it as a proxy for service quality. "Cream skimming" is the selection of clients who will be easier or cheaper for a service provider to utilize.

This same indicator can also be used to assess the impact on redistribution. It is usually supposed that those with greater needs or those who are more expensive or difficult to serve will be poorer or otherwise more disadvantaged. Adverse selection might happen given the incentive of cost saving. Marginalization of user groups should be avoided.

Volunteer

Concerning the impact on volunteering, there have been mutually contradictory possibilities of the development in practitioner and academic literatures. On the one hand, there is argument that voluntary organizations will increase their use and even exploitation of volunteers in order to undercut their pro-profit competitors. On the other hand, the concern that contracting will lead to professionalisation such that volunteers will be squeezed out is also raised. How volunteers perceive NGOs and the nature of their work and the relationship with the subvention reform and competitive bidding is critical.

Conclusion

In times of rapid changes of the welfare services in Hong Kong, we see an urgent need for a systematic enquiry for all the issues that we have mentioned earlier. Research studies and more genuine discussion between the NGOs and the government are deemed necessary.